They Might Be Saints

Michael O'Neill

They Might Be Saints
On the Path to Sainthood in America

EWTN PUBLISHING, INC.
Irondale, Alabama

EWTN Publishing, Inc.
5817 Old Leeds Road, Irondale, AL 35210

Distributed by Sophia Institute Press, Box 5284, Manchester, NH 03108.

paperback ISBN 978-1-68278-224-8
ebook ISBN 978-1-68278-225-5

Library of Congress Control Number: 2021944513

First printing

Contents

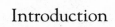

Introduction

When I returned home to Chicago after flying down to the EWTN network headquarters in Irondale, Alabama, in spring of 2016 to pitch a new television show concept related to my pseudonym, *The Miracle Hunter*, about investigating claims of the supernatural, I reflected on the generally warm reception but not full commitment of the Network to the project. I re-examined the future of this potential program and began to really scrutinize the nuts and bolts of the production—from storylines to budgets. There are a but a handful of places in the United States—such as the Church-approved apparitions of Our Lady of Good Help in Champion, Wisconsin, and the Santuario Chimayó and St. Joseph Staircase in New Mexico—that have a supernatural backstory worth recounting on television and even fewer that have any recognition or support from Rome. It made me ask the question: Who are the real miracle hunters in America? Who are the people whose job it is to identify a miracle and submit it to the Vatican for validation?

Very quickly the answer hit me over the head—it is the vice-postulators of American canonization causes who seek to identify scientifically-inexplicable healing miracles through the singular intercession of their would-be saints. These advocates work self-lessly and tirelessly to have their potential candidates for sainthood recognized by the Catholic Church. (Most of these vice-postulators are also members of the orders or congregations that were founded by or served in by the candidate.) Beyond the initial stage of getting the cause off the ground to the point of their candidate being named a "Servant of God" and therefore possibly someday being officially named a saint, the long and arduous task begins of collecting testimonies and examining in painstaking detail every aspect of the future saint's life. Their work is assembled in a *positio*, or academic position paper often hundreds of pages long, that makes the case for the worthiness of canonization of the future saint. When the pope authorizes the promulgation of a decree by the Vatican's Congregation for the Causes of Saints, thus recognizing a candidate's life of "heroic virtue," the candidate becomes known as "venerable" throughout the universal Catholic Church. Then and only then are intercessory miracles considered that will propel him or her to the next stages in the process: beatification after the first miracle is validated by the Congregation's Medical Commission and then canonization when a subsequent miracle is identified and found to be without natural explanation.

While it is commonly thought that the Vatican seeks out all cases of miracles and investigates each potentially legitimate one of them, the reality is that (other than at Lourdes) healing miracles are investigated and officially approved by the Catholic Church only when they are related to canonization causes. So it made good sense, then, to look to mold the television series around this well-established process and to create a series about Americans on the path to sainthood and the search for canonization miracles. Thus, the series *They Might Be Saints* was born.

I began to research the lives of future American saints and contact as many canonization causes as I could (there are almost one hundred active causes in the United States!) in order to gauge the interest of various people in collaborating with EWTN in order to produce programs that told the life stories of their candidates for sainthood. I found that there was almost universal interest in the project from the various guilds and organizations supporting a future saint, but I thought that the most interesting story of all of them involved a historic (i.e., longstanding with no living witnesses) sainthood cause run in the United States for a servant of God *not* from the United States. I pursued the fascinating story of Sr. Marie de Mandat-Grancey of France, a wealthy and saintly woman born in a castle who joined the Daughters of Charity in France and later was transferred to Turkey, where she followed the mystical writings of Bl. Anne Catherine Emmerich to find the house of the Virgin Mary where she lived with St. John in Ephesus. That fascinating episode was followed by programs on the Bishop Frederic Baraga, the "Snowshoe Priest" of Upper Peninsula, Michigan, the Martyrs of La Florida, and the story of Antonio Cuipa and companions, who were Apalachee Native Americans who converted to Catholicism through the Spanish but were martyred by the English. Numerous other episodes have followed, with the debut of the series on EWTN as a weekly program in March 2021, as have articles for the National Catholic Register and a "Might Be Saint-of-the-Day" segment on the "Miracle Hunter" radio program on EWTN Radio.

This book follows that trajectory with yet another opportunity for me to tell the stories of those people who have gone before us and walked amongst us on American soil, setting out a path for us to emulate in achieving holiness. This book highlights people born in the United States or who lived the majority of their lives in America. I hope that you find inspiration in your lives of faith as I have in getting to know these great models of living Christian virtue and that you seek their intercession for miracles and favors big and small as well.

Chapter 1

Sainthood

When we consider those holy people throughout history and wonder if *they might be saints* of the officially canonizable variety, perhaps it is important to reflect on what it means to be a saint in the first place. Whether we are talking about the types of people from an earlier era who seem to be the stuff of Catholic legends and the inspirations for the almost-mythical sounding stories of miracle workers and martyrs found in hagiographies throughout Christian history or, in more modern times, those ordinary people living extraordinary lives of heroic virtue, we can't help but look to the actual meaning of the word. "Saint" comes from the French derived from the Latin word *sanctus*, meaning "holy." In the Bible, the term "saint" is not used to denote members of the Church Triumphant in Heaven as Catholics have come to know it, but instead almost always refers to members of the Church Militant on earth, all the faithful who strive after a life of holiness. Early Christians regarded all the baptized as saints.

The *Catechism of the Catholic Church* (CCC) points out that members of the Catholic Church are considered part of the communion of saints:

> "Since all the faithful form one body, the good of each is communicated to the others.... We must therefore believe that there exists a communion of goods in the

Church. But the most important member is Christ, since he is the head.... Therefore, the riches of Christ are communicated to all the members, through the sacraments." "As this Church is governed by one and the same Spirit, all the goods she has received necessarily become a common fund." (947)

Beyond Scripture, the Catholic Church—and common parlance—uses the denotation "saint" to refer to any person who is in Heaven with God and will, after serious and oftentimes protracted study of their life of virtue, fame of sanctity, and verifiable intercessory miracles, add a new person worth emulating to the Church's official list or "canon" of saints. It is typically an arduous and lengthy canonization process, with the average length of the entire run from "Servant of God" to "Saint" being 181 years.[1] These recognized saints, having been "raised to the altars," are celebrated in the Church's liturgical life with each having been assigned a specific day as a solemnity, feast, obligatory memorial, or optional memorial and are highlighted as daily examples of holiness for us to follow.

The *Catechism of the Catholic Church* also explains the Church's historical practice of singling out certain individuals with the designation of saint:

> By *canonizing* some of the faithful, i.e., by solemnly proclaiming that they practiced heroic virtue and lived in fidelity to God's grace, the Church recognizes the power of the Spirit of holiness within her and sustains the hope of believers by proposing the saints to them as models and

---

[1] See Joe Drape, "The Poor Kansas Farm Boy Who Could Be a Saint," CNN, December 10, 2020, https://www.cnn.com/2020/12/10/opinions/emil-kapaun-path-to-sainthood-drape/.

intercessors. "The saints have always been the source and origin of renewal in the most difficult moments in the Church's history." Indeed, "holiness is the hidden source and infallible measure of her apostolic activity and missionary zeal." (828)

More than ten thousand saints are venerated in the Catholic Church. Since 1588, considering both martyrs and non-martyrs, 80 percent of all beatifications and canonizations have involved Europeans, with Spain, Italy, and France leading the way. A large number of martyrs makes Asia (15 percent) the second most common continent for saintly people recognized by the Church, while North America, South America, and Africa each represent approximately 1.5 percent of the overall tally. Although the trend is equalizing and even reversing in more modern times, more than three-fourths (75 percent) of blesseds and saints are men. A similar percentage of these declarations involve martyrs—those who died out of hatred for the Faith (Latin: *in odium fidei*)—compared to the one-quarter of saints and blesseds who are known as "confessors." In the span of centuries from 1588–1963, 90 percent of those recognized by Rome were priests or religious but, in the ensuing years, 75 percent have been lay members of the Christian faithful. These numbers are skewed, however, by the 2013 canonization by Pope Francis of 812 laypersons as the Martyrs of Oranto in southern Italy, where Antonio Primaldo and companions were killed in the year 1480 by Ottoman Turks after their refusal to convert to Islam.

During the pontificate of Pope Francis through 2020, the average age of a saint at death was just under sixty years old (59.77 years of age), with the Fátima siblings St. Francisco (age ten) and St. Jacinta Marto (age nine) being the youngest persons ever canonized. Two Americans, Bl. Miriam Teresa Demjanovich of New Jersey (1901–1927) and Bl. Michael McGivney of Connecticut (1852–1890), were at the times of their beatifications two of the five youngest people to be beatified by Pope Francis.[2]

Paths to Sainthood

In May 2007, Pope Benedict XVI issued the document *Sanctorum Mater* (Instruction for Conducting Diocesan or Eparchial Inquiries in the Causes of Saints) that denoted the three principal criteria for starting a sainthood cause: martyrdom, heroic virtue, and reputation for holiness. Popes may on their own initiative recognize someone as a saint in an "equivalent canonization after a long-standing *cultus* (veneration) and reputation for miracles is established. There are currently more than two thousand candidates for sainthood being evaluated in Rome.[3]

Martyrdom

Named for the Greek word for "witness," martyrs from the earliest days of Christianity, starting with St. Stephen (d. 33–36), gave up their lives for Christ. There are instances even of people in the territory that is (or became) the present-day United States who have died for the Faith:

- North American Martyrs
- Martyrs of La Florida, Georgia, and Virginia
- Bl. Stanley Rother (1935–1981) and Bl. James Miller (1944–1982)

---

[2] Data analyzed from "Saints and Blesseds of the Catholic Church," GCatholic.org, http://www.gcatholic.org/saints.

[3] See Msgr. Robert J. Sarno, "Steps to Sainthood," Congregation for the Causes of Saints, Fr. Solanus Guild, Capuchin Province of St. Joseph, https://solanuscasey.org/about-us/the-cause-for-sainthood/learn-more-about-the-steps-to-sainthood.

Heroic Virtue

When a saint is canonized, the implication is not that these people called "holy" lived a life of absolute perfection and never sinned. According to Catholic belief, only Jesus and Mary were conceived without Original Sin and were perfect. The term "heroic virtue" refers to the person's effort to overcome temptation and inclination to sin.

Some saints in fact were great sinners who struggled for years to overcome their moral failings. In the mold of St. Augustine of Hippo (354–430), who famously had an arduous and often tumultuous path of conversion, many others like Bl. Bartolo Longo (1841–1926), who was a high priest of Satan, St. Mary of Egypt (344–421), who was a seductress, and St. Olga of Kiev (d. 969), who was a mass murderer, are all examples of people who found holiness after lives of serious sin.

Oblatio Vitae

With his 2017 document *Maiorem hac dilectionem* ("Greater love than this"), Pope Francis by *motu proprio* (papal prerogative) added a new fourth path to sainthood: *oblatio vitae*, the giving up of one's life out of love for another, derived from the Scripture passage "Greater love has no man than this, that a man lay down his life for his friends" (John 15:13). An ordinary assembly of the Congregation for the Causes of Saints in 2014, followed by a complementary study initiated by Pope Francis in 2016, led to an open debate in which a majority of fifteen experts of the Congregation favored the new path, resulting in the approval of these provisions in a plenary session of cardinals and bishops.[4]

---

[4] See Antoine Mekary, "Giving Your Life for Another Can Lead to Canonization, Pope Decides," Aleteia, July 11, 2017, https://

The criteria established for this new path are these:
1. Free and voluntary offering of one's life, and heroic acceptance *propter caritatem* (Latin: "motivated by charity") of certain imminent death
2. Direct link between the offering of one's life and premature death
3. Exercise, at least to an ordinary degree, of Christian virtues before offering one's life, and after, until death
4. Existence of the reputation of sanctity and signs thereof, at least after death
5. Need of a beatification miracle through his or her intercession

Although this new path may appear to be similar to martyrdom due to the loss of life, it is distinct in that the violence of martyrdom is due to "hatred of the Faith," while a "heroic act of charity" is what precedes death in the other scenario. The precedence for this path to sainthood is found in the canonization of the "martyr of charity," St. Maximilian Kolbe, who offered himself as a replacement for a condemned prisoner in Auschwitz.

Equivalent Canonization

Waiving the need for a second miracle, the pope may simply confirm — not introduce — the longstanding *cultus* of a holy person and elevate them from blessed to saint through "equivalent" (or "equipollent") canonization. Initiated by Pope Urban VIII in 1632, this has happened throughout history in numerous cases, typically for seemingly long-forgotten saints of an earlier

---

aleteia.org/2017/07/11/giving-your-life-for-another-can-lead-to-canonization-pope-decides/.

era. There is typically no special ceremony in Rome for such a declaration.

Candidates for equipollent canonization must meet three criteria. They must be the subject of a long-standing cult. They should have a solid and enduring reputation for virtue. They must also have a long association with miracles. Such was the case with St. Margaret of Castello (1287–1320), canonized according to this path by Pope Francis in 2021.

While there were few equipollent canonizations in the twentieth century, the twenty-first century has seen some noteworthy ones, such as the first Jesuit priest, Peter Faber (1506–1546), and Angela of Foligno (1248–1309), both recognized by Pope Francis in 2013, and Hildegard of Bingen (1098–1179), recognized by Pope Benedict XVI in 2012.

Canonizations in the twenty-first century follow a long and detailed process that has been in development throughout the history of Christianity.

Early Christianity

Following the Roman persecutions of the early followers of Jesus, these martyrs as early as the second century were honored and remembered through public veneration on their death anniversaries. In the earliest years of Christianity, dying in witness of the Faith was seen as the epitome of holiness. Local cults venerating the early martyrs arose by public acclamation with no formal inquiries or declarations. A popular, widely accepted reputation for holiness could result in sainthood.

St. Cyprian (d. 258) called for investigation into the lives of martyrs before honoring them in this way. St. Augustine (d. 430) proposed that the duty fell to local bishops to investigate martyrdoms in their area.

It wasn't until the fourth century that "confessors"—those who lived heroically virtuous lives with a reputation for miracles—were recognized as saints. Ways that such Christians were identified and venerated included the placing of an altar over the saint's tomb, translating their relics to a church or other place of honor, promoting prayers that sought their intercession, and celebrating a local feast day.

Middle Ages

For centuries, it was the local bishop who would declare someone as a saint for veneration by that local region or nation. With the increasing requests by bishops for popes to intervene in the proclamation of a saint to give greater recognition and elevation to the candidate from the highest authority, the involvement of the papacy in the process increased.[5] A movement toward universal standards and centralization lead to a more formalized process. It wasn't until 993, when St. Ulrich (893–973), bishop of Augsburg, was declared a saint by Pope John XV (d. 996), that someone's holiness was recognized by the Holy See for the universal Church. Episcopal canonizations persisted for some time, with St. Walter of Pontoise (ca. 1030–ca. 1099) being raised to the altars by the bishop of Rouen in France in 1153. Pope Alexander III (ca. 1100–1181) by official decree in 1170 determined that going forward all saints would be designated by papal authority, and in 1243 Pope Gregory IX (ca. 1145–1241) confirmed this new standard with the proclamation that only a pope had the authority to declare someone a saint.

[5] See Fr. Richard Gribble, "How Does the Canonization Process Work?," Simply Catholic, https://simplycatholic.com/saints-in-the-christian-tradition/.

Canonizations after 1588

Pope Sixtus V (1521–1590) created the Congregation of Rites in 1588, establishing the processes of beatification and canonization. Responding to the centuries-old practice of potential saints being honored in their local regions, Pope Urban VIII (1568–1644) published a decree forbidding their public *cultus* or veneration until their martyrdom or heroic virtues had been formally recognized by the Congregation.

From the Eighteenth Century

The Italian Cardinal Prospero Lambertini (1675–1758) — the future Pope Benedict XIV — elaborated in 1740, in *De Servorum Dei Beatificatione et de Beatorum Canonizatione*, on the previous procedural norms issued by Pope Urban VIII (1568–1644), which forbade any form of public veneration, including the publication of books of miracles or revelations attributed to a potential saint, until their beatification or canonization.

In the twentieth century, the canonization process was further refined and centralized. The Code of Canon Law of 1917 codified the canonization process with 143 canons that dealt with beatification and canonization.

Pope St. Paul VI (1897–1978), in March 1969, split the Sacred Congregation of Rites into the Congregation for the Causes of Saints and the Congregation for Divine Worship. He simplified by *motu proprio* the norms for beatification in *Sanctitas clarior*, whereby a pope would have the diocesan bishop initiate a singular process after Rome's approval rather than requiring the informative process to run on both the local and Vatican levels. Further streamlining resulted in only an episcopal process becoming necessary to investigate the candidate's writings, life of virtue, martyrdom, public *cultus*, and purported miracles.

From 1983

Further advancements in the canonization process to make it simpler, faster, and less expensive occurred under the papacy of Pope St. John Paul II (1920–2005). Canonization causes are expensive — typically costing several hundred thousand dollars — due to the required manpower to read and manage the reports of miraculous cures and hire medical experts to examine potential cases. Some lives of would-be saints do not get examined due to the lack of an official sponsor or requisite funds.

The new inherent efficiencies made the Congregation more productive as well, resulting in Pope St. John Paul II being dubbed "the Great Saintmaker" for his record-setting number of canonizations and beatifications. While the new Code of Canon Law of 1983 was released with only one canon (1403) related to canonization, his apostolic constitution *Divinus Perfectionis Magister* reformed the entirety of the seventeenth-century sainthood process of Pope Urban VIII.

Pope John Paul II also abolished the "Devil's Advocate" (Latin: *advocatus diaboli*), replacing it with the "Promoter of Justice" (Latin: *promotor iustitiae*), a position that raises questions and possible objections to the advancement to sainthood and examines the accuracy of the inquiry on the saintliness of the candidate.

The requirement of two to four miracles for beatification and two to four miracles for canonization was changed to one miracle being necessary for each stage.

Modern Canonization Process

There are four stages for the canonization in the Catholic Church: servant of God, venerable, blessed, and saint.

1. Servant of God

The beginnings of the sainthood process are on the local level in the area where the candidate lived and was known, after a waiting period of five years after their death. The cause is initiated by a petitioner, or "actor," and is usually set up in the place where the person died (or sometimes in Rome). This petitioner, or "actor," may be an individual or a group (e.g., a religious congregation, diocese, association of lay faithful, parish, or civil body) with the interest and financial backing to promote the cause. Relevant documentation and information are collected and given to the local bishop, except in rare cases in which the candidate died outside of the bishop's territorial jurisdiction, in which case he would have to obtain the decree for transferring the case to him in order to become the competent bishop. Once the bishop examines the case, he may request starting an official investigation into the life of the person being considered for sainthood.

If the bishop determines that the canonization cause is worthy of further study, he will appoint a representative who is a lawyer to interact with Rome, a "postulator" who is an expert in theology, canon law, and history, with knowledge of the workings of the Congregation for the Causes of the Saints (CCS). A small number of Roman postulators handle nearly all the American sainthood causes. Some religious orders have postulators who work on all the international cases of potential saints from their order.

The competent bishop must consult with his region's bishops about the cause and publish the postulator's petition to the Vatican in order to induce the faithful to submit any relevant information about the potential saint. Once a cause is officially opened, the candidate receives the title "Servant of God." The CCS then designates a protocol number to refer to the case.

2. Venerable

Once the cause is officially initiated and the Diocesan Phase begins, theologians examine all the known writings of the servant of God and must provide a favorable opinion in order for the cause to proceed. The bishop then has a questionnaire for witnesses made up by the promoter of justice whom he assigns to the case. The CCS must also issue a *nihil obstat* to establish that there are no Vatican records that contain material that would later necessitate the suspension of the investigation.

A diocesan tribunal will examine the results of the investigations and historical research, including interviews with available witnesses and experts, and then a recommendation is made on the worthiness of the candidate to be canonized on the basis of virtue. The tribunal will submit their findings to the local bishop, who will ultimately decide if the results of the investigation merit being sent to the Vatican. While documentation from potential intercessory miracles may be collected at this point, there is no process at this point of validating medical cures until it has been demonstrated that the candidate has lived a life of heroic virtue and has been declared venerable by Rome.

The CCS validates the records of the investigation and appoints a *relator*, who supervises the writing and publication of the *positio super virtutibus* (referred to simply as a "positio"), an academic position paper compiled by a collaborator (typically the vice-postulator) summarizing the life and virtues of the servant of God. This document of several hundred pages contains both a biography of the servant of God and a summary (Latin: *summarium*) of all the testimonies of the witnesses and documents relative to the candidate's life. A theological commission of historians, theologians, and prelates appointed by the CCS then reviews this material and votes affirmatively or negatively to determine the final result of the cause. If affirmative, it is then passed to the bishop-members of the Congregation, who vote to determine whether it be recommended that the pope promulgate the decree of heroic virtue for a particular person, thereby officially recognizing the servant of God's life of heroic virtue and establishing them as venerable.

Venerables do not have a feast day assigned to them and cannot have churches named for them since, with this decree, the Church has declared that they are *worthy of Heaven* but not that they are *definitively in Heaven*. The faithful are encouraged —through prayer cards, websites, and the activities of guilds—to pray for the saintly person's canonization and intercession. The identification and verification of a medical miracle displaying the person's intercessory power would prove to the Vatican that the person is indeed in Heaven.

3. Beatification

Beatification—resulting in a candidate being termed blessed—is the penultimate step in the process of canonization and the Catholic Church's official certification that the person is in Heaven with God. Prior to the candidate being "raised to the altars," the previous step—the declaration that a person is venerable—established that the candidate, in the eyes of the Church after much scrutiny and investigation, lived a life *worthy of Heaven* but cannot be guaranteed to be *in Heaven*. Except in the cases of martyrdom, beatification requires the recognition that the person has interceded for a verifiable miracle.

During the pontificate of John Paul II and departing from earlier tradition, beatifications normally took place in Rome, where the pope himself could officiate at the ceremony. On some occasions, he celebrated this rite in the country where the blessed was born, lived, or died. In one particularly meaning-ful example, for the 1990 beatification of St. Juan Diego, the visionary of the apparitions of Our Lady of Guadalupe, John Paul II traveled to Mexico City to celebrate a Mass attended by millions of faithful. Under Pope Benedict XVI and Pope Francis, the head of the Congregation for the Causes of Saints or another cardinal appointed by the pope has presided over the rite in the local region.

After the ceremony of beatification takes place, the venerable is now referred to as a blessed (in Latin: *beatus* or *beata*). Only now may a feast day be established, to be observed only in the blessed's home diocese and within his or her religious community (where applicable). Parishes are typically not named in honor of a blessed (perhaps for practical reasons related to signage and the inherent hope of them being soon declared a saint), but modern exceptions have been made for Mother Teresa and John Paul II. Official shrines in honor of the blessed are erected for the faith-ful to come and venerate their relics and seek their intercession for blessings, favors, graces, and the ever-elusive second miracle that will propel them to being declared a saint.

4. Canonization

For canonization, an approved second miracle is required by the Vatican that occurs *after* the official promulgation of the decree of beatification. This is both a matter of allowing Heaven to ratify, in a sense, the Church's decision of a person being acknowledged as a blessed and then a saint and also a matter of practicality: theoretically, if a cause had two miracles (instead of just the one) pre-identified and pre-validated by the Medical Commission, it could "play two cards at once" and skip the beatification process altogether and jump ahead to canonization.

After the Congregation for the Causes of Saints promulgates a decree of a second miracle that will lead to the candidate being declared a saint, the pope will hold an Ordinary Public Consistory as the last step before the canonization can take place. At this consistory, cardinals resident or present in Rome will vote to approve the canonization of one or more candidates. This is the final step in the sainthood process and allows a date to be set for a Mass of canonization.

Once the canonization Mass takes place, the servant of God will then be acknowledged as a saint by the universal Church and may be celebrated with a feast day on the General Roman Calendar.

Chapter 2

Miracles in Canonizations

It may surprise many people that the Vatican does not employ a team of miracle investigators who get sent out around the world when credible reports of medical miracles make their way to Rome of a potentially supernatural event, such as the spontaneous healing of a stage-four cancer victim or the recovery of eyesight for a person stricken with blindness. Vatican officials might certainly encourage and model a position of gratitude to God for each time one of the faithful receives such a monumental and faith-inspiring blessing from God, but there would be no resulting activity on their part. Other than at Lourdes—the famed French site of Marian apparitions received by a fourteen-year-old visionary, St. Bernadette Soubirous, and its resulting healing spring that still produces miracles that are formally examined by a medical bureau—the only place of investigation of healing miracles in the entire Catholic world is the Congregation for the Causes of Saints, which examines medical cures being proposed by postulators of canonization causes as proofs of the intercessory power of their potential saint. Such a verified miracle establishes the saint's presence in Heaven and therefore merits formal recognition by the Catholic Church.

In addition to the years (often spans of decades or even centuries in older cases) in which the causes for canonization gather testimonies and documentation attesting to the potential saint's life of virtue and assemble information pointing to the candidate's fame of sanctity in life and in death, the causes search for verifiable miracles worked through the intercession of their singular saint. There have been saints known for "thaumaturgy" (from Greek: "wonderworking"), having worked many miracles during their lives, but none of these can be used toward the miracle requirement, as they do not establish the person as a saint in Heaven enjoying the Beatific Vision. If a posthumous miracle is approved as authentic (and it can be shown that the recipient had an established devotion to that particular saint and sought the help of no other to obtain a certain favor), that is a clear sign to Rome that the potential saint is truly in Heaven and close to God interceding for this blessing. According to Catholic belief, it is not possible that a person in Purgatory or Hell would be able to intercede for a miracle in response to the prayers of the faithful on earth.

The vast majority of miracles proposed in sainthood causes are medical cures because of the strong documentation of the illness that exists before the healing and the verification that happens afterward. While it is possible that something other than a medical miracle might be used in a canonization, such instances are extremely rare. One such case involved food multiplication. In Extremadura, Spain, poor families and orphaned children would come to the Ribera del Fresno parish hall each evening for a meal. On January 25, 1949, when it became clear that for the day's meal there was not enough food for everyone, with less than a pound and a half each of meat and rice available, the cook prayed in desperation to Bl. John Macias (1585–1645), who was from that area and had cared for the poor there. Twenty-two people testified that the pot began overflowing and the cook needed two more pots to hold the extra. Over the course of four hours, the food kept coming with over two hundred people being fed.[6]

Another non-medical miracle case is attributed to Bl. Irene Stefani, an Italian nun given the name "Sr. Nyaatha" ("Mother of Mercy") by the Kenyan people whom she served in hospitals. She was beatified under Pope Francis on May 23, 2015, and her miracle involved keeping a holy water font full in a parish church in Mozambique in 1989, as it was the only water source for a group of refugee catechists who were hiding from warring liberation armies.[7]

Canonization causes will try to collect documentation for as many miracles as possible and some less dramatic examples of intercession for their would-be saint—often termed "favors," "blessings," or "graces"—that would likely not pass muster from Rome. From these, the best examples are selected and examined by medical experts on the diocesan level, often at great expense to the cause. If there appears to be reasonable hope of it meeting the Vatican's high miracle standards, at the suggestion of the cause's postulator, it will be sent to Rome to be reviewed and validated. For the causes of some saints reputed as "wonderworkers," such as Detroit's Bl. Solanus Casey and Montreal's St. André Bessette, their promoters flooded the approval process with numerous

---

6   See Randall Sullivan, *The Miracle Detective: An Investigation of Holy Visions* (New York: Atlantic Monthly Press, 2004), cited in "No Miracles Allowed: Historical/Critical Exegesis," *Metaphysical Catholic* (blog), June 16, 2011, http://metaphysicalcatholic. blogspot.com/2011/06/no-miracles-required-historicalcritical. html.
7   See "Blessed Irene Stefani," CatholicSaints.Info, July 1, 2016, https://catholicsaints.info/blessed-irene-stefani/.

claims to be considered.[8] A collection of miracles, it might be thought, might assist in the establishment of the person's reputation for holiness and intercessory power.

In *De Servorum Dei Beatificatione et de Beatorum Canonizatione*, Prospero Lambertini (1675–1758), the future Pope Benedict XIV, argued that the potentially miraculous events proposed as instances of saintly intercessions in canonization causes must present themselves to human reason as being truly extraordinary and be without natural explanation.

Cures must meet seven criteria to be considered miraculous:

1. The disease must be serious and impossible (or at least very difficult) to cure by medical intervention;
2. The disease must not be in a stage at which it is liable to disappear on its own;
3. There must be no medical treatment given that is related to the cure;
4. The cure must be spontaneous;
5. The cure must be complete;
6. The cure must be lasting;
7. The cure must not be produced by another disease or crisis of a sort that would make it possible that the cure was wholly or partially natural.

In cases of the cure of life-threatening illnesses, it had been required that someone with a healing pass away from another cause in order to guarantee that the disease did not return. There is now in standard practice a five-year waiting period for cancer-victims before their healing is considered to have been a miracle. In the cause of Bl. Francis Xavier Seelos of New Orleans, which

---

8 See Patricia Treece, *Nothing Short of a Miracle* (Manchester, NH: Sophia Institute Press, 2013), xxv–xxvi.

was seeking a second miracle to lead to his canonization, a woman with a cure from cancer through his intercession died of pneumonia before the required five years had passed, so her miracle was not able to be used.[9]

A *positio super miraculo* for the proposed miracle is assembled and sent to Rome with all the testimonies and medical documentation of the investigation spearheaded by an uninvolved doctor appointed by the local bishop. The case is reviewed by a panel from the medical consultation team of the Congregation for the Causes of Saints, composed of sixty doctors in various specialties who have no connection to the cases on which they render judgments.

In 2016, Pope Francis approved revised norms for the medical consultation team of the Congregation for the Causes of Saints for any declaration on a healing with no natural or scientific explanation. The Congregation first reviews the presumed miracle with two medical experts, and at their recommendation it is sent to the medical consultation team. The medical panel, comprised of a maximum of seven experts (unknown to the postulator), is required to have a quorum of six experts with a two-thirds majority needed to make a positive judgment. Previously, only the approval of a simple majority of the consultation team members present was required. When the promoter of a cause appeals a negative judgment, the new norms state that a new team of physicians and medical experts must be appointed, but an alleged miracle "cannot be re-examined more than three times."

In the beatification process for St. Katharine Drexel (1858–1955) of Philadelphia, her cause examined the cure of a boy, Robert Gutherman, who had lost hearing on one side due to a

---

[9] Treece, *Nothing Short of a Miracle,* xxxii.

serious infection that ate away the bones in his ear. Despite his hearing having returned after the prayers of his family to the saintly nun and the bones in his ear having been miraculously restored, Gutherman's hearing was examined into adulthood to establish the permanence of the cure. His cure inspired prayers in another case of hearing loss, when two-year-old Amy Wall was miraculously healed in 1994 of nerve deafness through then-Bl. Katherine Drexel's intercession. The investigation resulted in a seven hundred-page *positio* covering the lifetime medical history of the girl, interviews with doctors, testimonies from friends and relatives about the details of her condition and her speed of recovery, and the specifics of how her intercession was sought to establish a pre-existing history of devotion and seeking out a singular saint. Passing the review of the medical bureau as being without natural explanation, the report of the cure was passed on to the board of nine theological reviewers, who examined the details of the requested intercession.

After a medical healing is identified and verified as being without known natural cause, it is then looked at by theologians who try to assess whether the miracle is due to supernatural factors, specifically the intercession of the saint in question. One of the most challenging aspects of identifying a worthy miracle is first establishing that it was worked *exclusively* through the intercession of the would-be saint. It is reasonable to think that a person in serious need of aid would ask many people for their assistance, but in the sainthood process it is important to identify a strong pre-existing devotion and targeted prayers to that specific saint in order that singular intercession might be established. Only in very rare cases, such as that of the Fátima siblings, Jacinta and Francisco Marto, who were canonized together on the Fátima centenary, on May 13, 2017, or the parents of St. Thérèse of Lisieux—Louis and Zélie Martin—who, in 2015, became the first married couple to be canonized together, does the Catholic Church allow multiple people to be sought out in prayer for a canonization miracle.

After that, the cause and its miracle claim are evaluated by a special commission of cardinals and bishops, who review the findings of the doctors and theologians. If everything checks out, it is passed to the desk of the pope, who signs off on the case in an official act of authentication. Not until science, faith, and the authority of the Church are behind it will a miracle be considered a proof to be used in a candidate's beatification or canonization.

In order for the blessed to then be canonized, a miracle *after* the beatification must be identified. Perhaps this is to demonstrate Heaven's assent to the proceedings for that particular saint or to prevent a canonization cause from stockpiling their miracles and attempting to very quickly progress through the steps. The quickest a second miracle has ever been allowed must have been in the case of St. John Paul II, when a Costa Rican woman with one month to live was healed of a brain aneurysm through his intercession on May 1, 2011, while praying to him while watching his beatification ceremony on television. This was the very miracle that led to his canonization.

Prior to St. John Paul II's pontificate, two to four miracles were required for beatification and the same number for canonization. Since 1983, the Church has used this more streamlined process, bringing forth more saintly role models for the world to see. In a 2006 papal letter, Pope Benedict XVI insisted that candidates in the saint-making process must "truly enjoy a firm and widespread reputation for holiness." In addition, he insisted on the need for a candidate to be the verified intercessor of "a physical miracle, since a moral miracle does not suffice." Such an occurrence is a "signal from God" in the form of a miracle to ratify the Church's positive judgment on the virtuous life of a candidate.

From 2000 to 2020, nine miracles have been approved by the Vatican in American sainthood causes:

2000 — Pope John Paul II approved the promulgation of a decree from the Congregation for the Causes of Saints that two-year-old Amy Wall was miraculously healed in 1994 of nerve deafness in both ears through the intercession of St. Katharine Drexel (1858–1955), which lead to her canonization.

2004 — After receiving the unanimous affirmation from the Congregation for the Causes of Saints, Pope John Paul II approved as a miracle a 1992 medical cure that involved Kate Mahoney, a fourteen-year-old New York girl who recovered from multiple organ failure after friends and family prayed with a relic for the intercession of St. Marianne Cope (1838–1918).

2006 — Pope Benedict XVI approved the promulgation of the decree that the 2001 cure of the failing eyesight of an Indiana man, Phil McCord, through the intercession of St. Théodore Guérin (1798–1856), was indeed a miracle.

2008 — The miraculous recovery in 1999 through the intercession of St. Damien of Molokai (1840–1889) of Audrey Toguchi, a Hawaiian woman with metastasized liposarcoma, a terminal cancer that arises in fat cells, was approved by Pope Benedict XVI.

2011 — Pope Benedict XVI signed and approved the promulgation of the decree of a miracle received by

Sharon Smith, a sixty-five-year-old woman from Chittenango, New York, who was healed from pancreatitis in 2005 through the intercession of St. Marianne Cope (1838–1918).

2011—Pope Benedict XVI approved the second miracle needed for the canonization of Kateri Tekakwitha (1656–1680) when Jake Finkbonner, a young boy in Washington state, survived a severe flesh-eating bacterium in 2006.

2013—Pope Francis approved the attribution of miraculous restoration in 1963 of perfect vision to an eight-year-old boy, Michael Mencer, who had gone legally blind because of macular degeneration, through the intercession of Bl. Miriam Teresa Demjanovich (1901–1927).

2017—The Congregation for the Causes of Saints and Pope Francis approved a miracle involving the 2012 cure of Paula Medina Zarate of Panama from ichthyosis, a genetic skin condition, attributed to Bl. Solanus Casey, which led to his beatification that took place at Ford Field in Detroit in front of an estimated crowd of sixty thousand.

2020—The miraculous cure from fetal hydrops—an uncommon, typically fatal condition where fluid builds up around the vital organs of an unborn child—attributed to the intercession of Bl. Michael McGivney was approved by the Congregation for the Causes of Saints and authorized by Pope Francis.

Chapter 3

American Saints: An Overview

With the United States being a relatively young country compared with the traditionally Catholic nations of Europe and elsewhere, there are very few canonized American saints, especially considering the total number of saints in Church history to be over ten thousand. Through the end of the twentieth century, there had only been eleven canonizations of people who were born, died, or spent significant time in the United States (or in the territories that were to someday become the United States).

From New York to Hawaii, below is the short list of American saints:

Saint Isaac Jogues (January 10, 1607–October 18, 1646) and the North American Martyrs

French Jesuit missionaries and martyrs, they ministered among the Iroquois, Huron, and other Native populations in North America. The North American Martyrs, which consisted of St. Isaac Jogues (1646), St. René Goupil (1642), St. Jean de Lalande (1646), St. Antoine Daniel (1648), St. Jean de Brébeuf (1649), St. Noël Chabanel (1649), St. Charles Garnier (1649), and St. Gabriel Lalemant (1649), were canonized in 1930 by Pope Pius XI. Their feast day is October 18.

Saint Kateri Tekakwitha (1656–April 17, 1680)

Known as the "Lily of the Mohawks," the Algonquin-Mohawk laywoman was born in Ossernenon, a Mohawk village near present-day Auriesville, New York. After converting to Catholicism and taking a vow of perpetual virginity, she moved to a Jesuit mission in Quebec. She was the first Native American to be canonized, in 2012, by Pope Benedict XVI. Her feast day is July 14.

Saint Junípero Serra, O.F.M.
(November 24, 1713–August 28, 1784)

Born in Majorca, Spain and arriving in Mexico in 1749, the founder of the first nine of twenty-one missions spanning from San Diego to San Francisco earned himself the title of the "Apostle of California." He was the first person canonized on American soil, in 2015, at the Basilica of the National Shrine of the Immaculate Conception by Pope Francis. His feast day is July 1.

Saint Rose Philippine Duchesne
(August 29, 1769–November 18, 1852)

An early member of the Religious Sisters of the Sacred Heart of Jesus, she was a French religious sister who taught and served the people on the Western frontier of the United States and died in Missouri. She was canonized in 1988 by Pope John Paul II, and her feast day is November 18.

Saint Elizabeth Ann Seton
(August 28, 1774–January 4, 1821)

The first saint born in what is now the United States, she became known as a founder of the country's parochial school system, establishing the nation's first girls' school in Emmitsburg,

Maryland. She also started the first American congregation of religious sisters, the Sisters of Charity. She was canonized in 1975 by Pope Paul VI, and her feast day is January 4.

Saint Théodore Guérin (October 2, 1798–May 14, 1856)

Foundress of the Sisters of Providence of St. Mary of the Woods, she was a French religious sister who founded numerous schools in Indiana and eastern Illinois and is known for her care of the orphaned, the sick, and the poor. Pope Benedict XVI canonized her in 2006, and her feast day is October 3.

Saint John Nepomucene Neumann (March 28, 1811–January 5, 1860)

Immigrating from Bohemia as a priest in 1836, he became the fourth bishop of Philadelphia and is known as the founder of diocesan school systems in the United States. He became the first male saint from the United States, canonized by Pope Paul VI in 1977. His feast day is January 5.

Saint Damien de Veuster (January 3, 1840–April 15, 1889)

Known simply as Fr. Damien, as a missionary priest he ministered for eleven years to the leper colony on the Hawaiian island of Molokai. The Apostle of the Lepers cared for the patients and worked with the community to build houses, schools, roads, hospitals, and churches. He was canonized in 2009 by Pope Benedict XVI, and his feast day is May 10.

Saint Frances Xavier Cabrini (July 15, 1850–December 22, 1917)

The patroness of immigrants and refugees, Mother Cabrini was the first American citizen to be made a saint. An Italian immigrant, she founded the Missionary Sisters of the Sacred Heart of Jesus, a religious institute that was a major support to her fellow Italian immigrants to the United States. She died in Chicago and was canonized in 1946 by Pope Pius XII. Her feast day is November 13.

Saint Marianne Cope, O.S.F.
(January 23, 1838–August 9, 1918)

A German religious sister who was a member of the Sisters of St. Francis of Syracuse, New York, she was a missionary with six other sisters who ministered starting in 1883 to leprosy patients on the island of Molokai in Hawaii. She was canonized in 2012 by Pope Benedict XVI, and her feast day is January 23.

Saint Katharine Drexel
(November 26, 1858–March 3, 1955)

Born in Philadelphia, she was an heiress, philanthropist, educator, and foundress (and superior) of the Sisters of the Blessed Sacrament, ministering to both African Americans and Native Americans. She was canonized in 2000 by Pope John Paul II and has her feast day on March 3.

⁂

With the large number of current servants of God (and more added each year) and numerous other active causes for American venerables and blesseds, the number of saints in the States will surely be on the rise in the years and decades to come. In the meantime, the short saint list provides the faithful with a strong set of intercessors and models from whom to seek inspiration.

Chapter 4

American Blesseds

Blessed Francis Xavier Seelos
The Happy Saint

Born: January 11, 1819 (Füssen, Germany)
Died: October 4, 1867 (New Orleans, Louisiana)
Venerated: January 27, 2000 (Pope John Paul II)
Beatified: April 9, 2000 (Pope John Paul II)
Feast Day: October 8

"This morning there departed from the diocesan seminary here one of its most worthy members, Francis Xavier Seelos (born in Füssen, 1819), to leave for North America, and there, after entering the Redemptorist Order in Baltimore, to dedicate himself for his entire life to the important vocation of a missionary. May the Lord accompany with superabundant blessing this truly apostolic undertaking." So read the *Augsburger Postzeitung* on December 9, 1842.

Until three weeks before, only Francis's father had known of his son's intention to become a priest in the United States. On one of their "walking trips," Francis had confided to Mang

New Orleans ★

Seelos his desire to be a missionary. Mang gave his blessing. It came as no surprise to Mang that his son had decided to be a priest. He had played Mass as a child and prayed the Rosary by himself after the family prayers. When he started school after a sickly childhood that it didn't seem he would live through, he proved himself one of the most brilliant pupils at the Füssen primary school.

Though Mang was a skilled weaver and had a small farm to provide for the basics, he couldn't afford to send Francis to secondary school. But with a scholarship from the town to cover tuition and incidentals, plus the help of the parish priest in arranging for his room and board, Francis was able to continue his education in Augsburg, about forty miles away. One family provided a bed and roof for the night, while other families gave the young student "meal days," a place at their table for the main midday meal. For breakfast and dinner, Francis usually munched on some bread. His parents also sent him a small allowance every week, but that went right through his hands. Anyone in need of money came to him. "Banker Seelos," they called him at school, except that he didn't keep accounts for repayment.

"They are poorer than I am and do not have any meal days or money," he explained to his parents when they heard what was going on. "I cannot stand seeing them go without, as long as I have something."

Francis had also inherited his father's jolly spirit and love for the outdoors and singing. At sung Masses, he would get so carried away with the music he practically shouted, oblivious to the remonstrations of his friends. On his vacations from school, he took long "walking trips" through the countryside shrines and minor pilgrimage churches. When he was sixteen, he walked fifteen hours to the Benedictine Monastery at Einsiedeln and asked to be admitted. The monks rejected him. He came home dejected but didn't, ultimately, change his intention to be a priest and religious. Still, when he graduated from high school, he decided not to go to the philosophy course offered by the Benedictines in Augsburg. Instead, he went on to the University of Munich on another scholarship from the Füssen Town Hall. He studied philosophy, but he was not in the seminary. Instead, he lived with two cousins and his brother, learned dancing, fencing, and violin, and became a connoisseur of tobacco, which he snuffed with relish.

He advanced to theology studies but still had not entered the seminary. In a dream one night, he saw himself as a priest at the altar, holding the consecrated host in his hand ready to give the congregation communion. Then he looked up, distracted by an "unusually attractive" young woman. He "immediately recommended her to God and strove only to know the will of his divine master." The appeals of the Redemptorists for missionaries in America also reached his ears.

"Today we will not write," he told his brother Adam, who was studying a trade in Munich and had come for his weekly writing lesson that Sunday in 1842. "Last night the Blessed Mother appeared to me. I have to be a missionary."

On his summer vacation, Francis told his father about his decision to be a missionary and applied to the Redemptorists in Maryland, though the two men decided it was best to keep it between themselves for the time being. Francis returned to Füssen in September, this time as a seminarian, the best way, he thought, to await the answer of the Redemptorists. As father and son said goodbye, Mang silently pointed to the sky. Francis understood the message. They would see each other again in Heaven. In November, Francis received his acceptance letter from the Redemptorists. Like his patron saint, he did not make a final visit home before leaving for the missions. Instead, he spent the months before his journey to America with the Redemptorists in Altötting and broke the news and said farewell to his family by letter.

"Even though I am far away, love remains and united us eternally here in prayer for one another. Love has united us, love does not mean parting, love will always remain, love will unite us again in the beyond," he wrote his sister Antonia, his confidant from childhood. "I am writing this not without tears and you will be crying too.... Farewell forever, dearest unforgettable sister!"

Francis set sail for America from La Havre on March 17, 1843, and landed in New York a month later on Holy Thursday. After a short stay with the Redemptorists in New York, Francis made his way to Baltimore for his novitiate. He made his first vows on May 16, 1844, and was ordained a priest at the parish church of St. James the Lesser six months later on December 22, 1844.

He spent his first eight months as a priest right there at St. James the Lesser in Baltimore. Released from the novitiate and seminary studies into the world of parish work, he was deeply encountering the differences between his Bavarian homeland and his American mission land. "The bedbugs, insects, the religious sects, the language and so many things more" were his chief annoyances. He would never, actually, preach easily in English. In America, he also found, reigned "the vulgar spirit of speculation, business, money, the coldness and dryness of the people — nowhere a cross or a church of pilgrimage — no happy faces, no songs, no singing, everything dead." Still, he was happy.

"Nonetheless, I love my life ... I am always as healthy as can be and do not want for the smallest thing — the best food, decent clothing. We have heat and water in the house, which can be used all through the night," he wrote home.

He was then transferred to St. Philomena Church in Pittsburgh, where Fr. John Neumann was pastor and superior. The future bishop and saint became a true guide to Fr. Seelos in the midst of demanding priestly duties. Here the Redemptorists had in their charge not only the main urban parish but also churches and outposts for a hundred miles around. Initially, the novitiate had been relocated to the parish, as well. The newly ordained took his complete portion of Masses and preaching near and far, confessions, visits to the sick, and catechism classes. He preached in English, German, and French. In Baltimore, Fr. Seelos had already made a reputation for himself as a homilist. He had a knack for explaining the Faith in simple terms applicable to his hearers, and his style was engaging, even entertaining. His homilies could be one-man shows where the characters from the Gospel quipped back and forth before he summarized the lessons of the day's Gospel. He usually ended with a heartfelt call for all to bring themselves to the mercy of God.

"Ah, you sinners," he would say, stretching his arms wide, "who have not the courage to confess your sins because they are so numerous or so grievous or so shameful. O, come without fear or trembling! I promise to receive you with all mildness. If I do not keep my word, I here publically [*sic*] give you permission to cast it up to me in the confessional and to charge me with a falsehood!"

The line outside his confessional was always long.

In 1848, he was, to his surprise, appointed novice master. It was a short-lived assignment, as the novitiate was transferred to Cumberland, Maryland, six months later. That same year, Fr. Seelos made his annual retreat and dug in even deeper into his spiritual life, committing himself more seriously than ever to reaching holiness in his vocation.

"As long as there is breath in me, and with your help and grace, I will never give up. I am fully prepared for everything and give my body, and my soul completely into your hands as a holocaust," he wrote in his retreat notes as the ten-day spiritual exercises began.

But it wasn't easy.

On the fourth day he wrote, "O help! O help! O holy Mother of God, let me become so inflamed and sanctified that I am not always thinking of breakfast."

Indeed, the life of a priest in America at that time could be a genuine sacrifice of body and soul. To the travel by horseback or foot to reach the furthest outposts was added sometimes with anti-Catholicism. Fr. Seelos had rocks pelted at him in the street, was beaten during a sick call, and was almost thrown overboard on a ferry when he knelt out of respect for the Blessed Sacrament he was carrying.

Neither his successive appointments as pastor of increasingly larger parishes nor the harshness of times could change his gentle disposition or his availability to everyone. He talked for half an hour with the poor woman or the half-witted man who came to the rectory for a meal. When a fellow brother chided him for wasting his time, Fr. Seelos replied simply that he could not receive some people kindly and others not. He kept vigil at the bed of a sick child so the mother could rest, and he did a pile of laundry for another poor woman sick in bed. He gave his gloves away to a poor man he passed on the street. No one was rushed out of the confessional. He sincerely wanted to hear the penitent's life story and see how he could best advise him. When visiting the sick, he took time for a friendly visit with the patient. He was known to sleep in his clothes near the door to more quickly answer the inevitable nighttime sick calls. His most famous sick call was the night he was asked to come to the local whorehouse for a dying prostitute. He didn't hesitate, even though he knew it would make the papers.

"Let them talk," he said. "I saved a soul!"

Eventually, his untiring ministry caught up to him. Like he did many days, he had been sitting in the confessional of St. Alphonsus Church in Baltimore for hours in the late winter cold. He stepped out, stretched, and started to exercise to get his blood moving. A stream of blood spewed out of his mouth. He had had a hemorrhage in his throat. He didn't complain, but his confreres could see that he was not well and wrote to the provincial superior that Fr. Seelos needed to see a doctor. He was hospitalized for a month.

Meanwhile, the Redemptorists were looking for a new prefect for their seminary. Under the previous prefect of students, the atmosphere had become morose and unhealthy. Their sights landed on Fr. Seelos, who came recommended as "a saint in spirituality and an angel in sweetness."

Fr. Seelos taught some of the theology classes and set the rhythm of life at the seminary. To prayer and study, he added walking trips and swimming at the beach in summer. He also allowed the seminarians to put on plays. Curious when he heard about it, he briefly joined the "Laughing Club" three of the students had formed. The rules were simple. At any given moment and without warning a member could be called on to make a joke, but no one was allowed to laugh until signaled by the joke-teller. Those who could not hold out got a penance. Fr. Seelos had to quickly leave the club, as, he complained, he was getting too many penances.

Though the number of seminarians had doubled, not all of the Redemptorists approved of Fr. Seelos or his innovations. Especially opposed was the priest he had replaced. The man's viperous letters, and those of others, to the congregation's highest authority in Rome finally prevailed. Fr. Seelos was notified without explanation that his replacement was being sent from Europe. He was not given the chance to defend himself against his detractors, either. Though it hurt, his response was a chatty letter to the superior general.

"The whole change went forward without any difficulty because all were happy to see it as the greatest of blessings and accepted the new prefect with gratitude ... I will be happy to go hand in hand with the new prefect and help him in whatever I can. It seems to me the choice could not have fallen on a better and more capable father," he wrote.

His ousting from the seminary landed Fr. Seelos in his favorite assignment of his priesthood—leader of a mission band. A nineteenth-century Redemptorist mission was the tent revival of Catholicism. Working in groups as small as two or as large as six, Redemptorists crisscrossed the United States from the East Coast to the Great Plains, taking parishes by storm and preaching, teaching, and hearing confessions for a week or so. They could spend up to twelve hours a day in the confessional. The mission revived and invigorated Catholics of all spiritual states and marked a spiritual high point for the community as whole. As Fr. Seelos wrote, one congregation was so enthused and grateful they nearly carried the priests off as if they had just won the World Series. For two years, from 1863–1865, he and five other Redemptorists preached and heard confessions through ten states from New York to Missouri. Fr. Seelos was in his element.

"I love the mission more than anything else," he wrote to his sister. "It is properly the work of the vineyard of the Lord."

After his time on the mission trail, he was sent back to parish ministry, first briefly to Detroit, Michigan, and then to New Orleans. With its hot, humid climate perfect for breeding infectious diseases, its pockets of poverty, and the influx of people through its port, New Orleans had a reputation as dangerous place. Fr. Seelos calmly foresaw that here his life would end.

"I will be there one year and then I will die of yellow fever," he told a School Sister of Notre Dame whom he chatted with on the journey to his last parish.

That is exactly what happened. For one year, he continued as he always had—humble, especially kind to the poor and sick, consoling sinners in Confession, encouraging Catholics from the pulpit, and available to everyone, until the yellow fever epidemic struck in 1867. Fr. Seelos ignored his first symptoms, of course. His superior sent him to bed. Initially, it seemed he would pull through. The fever had passed, but he was still languishing three weeks later. Then he worsened again. The infirmarian asked if he had any matters of family inheritance that needed to be settled.

"No," he smiled, "Before I came to America we settled everything. I get nothing and they also get nothing."

For the next few days, he went in and out of delirium. He would preach wildly in German and English and then fall asleep. Once, he woke up, suddenly, startled.

"Where am I? Am I dead?" he said.

The infirmarian laughed. Then Fr. Seelos did, too.

The morning of October 4 looked like it would be his last day on earth. His fellow priests and brothers circled around his bed and sang a Marian hymn that Seelos loved. He was visibly relieved, lifted up. He remained conscious to the end, murmuring prayers as his illness pushed him toward death. He died that evening.

⌒

PRAYER FOR THE INTERCESSION OF
BLESSED FRANCIS XAVIER SEELOS

O my God, I truly believe You are present with me. I adore Your limitless perfections. I thank You for the graces and gifts You gave to Bl. Francis Xavier Seelos. If it is Your holy will, please let him be declared a saint of the Church so that others may know and imitate his holy life. Through his prayers please give me this favor: (make your request).

⌒

Please report any miracles or favors to:

National Shrine of Blessed Francis Xavier Seelos
919 Josephine Street
New Orleans, LA 70130
(504) 525-2495
seelos.org
info@seelos.org

Blessed Michael McGivney

Parish Priest and Founder of the Knights of Columbus

Born: August 12, 1852 (Waterbury, Connecticut)
Died: August 14, 1890 (Thomaston, Connecticut)
Venerated: March 15, 2008 (Pope Benedict XVI)
Beatified: October 31, 2020 (Pope Francis)
Feast Day: August 13

Michael McGivney closed the sacristy door, went to the nave of the chapel, and knelt down to say the Rosary. The sacristan seminarian was happier at St. Mary's Seminary in Baltimore than he had expected to be, especially now that he was certain about the diocesan priesthood. With his intellectual, driven bent the Jesuits had naturally appealed to him. In fact, he had been attend-

ing the Jesuit St. Mary's College in Montreal before his father died. That tragedy had almost cost his vocation altogether. But when the Bishop of Hartford, Connecticut found out that this promising seminarian had lost the family support that was getting him through seminary, he offered Michael a full scholarship to the seminary in Baltimore. He certainly didn't want to lose this young man to the Jesuits, either. Diocesan priests were a commodity in America in the 1800s. They were too few, they worked hard, and all too often thye died young from catching the rampant infectious diseases that had brought them to a sick call or a death bed. Connecticut needed this star seminarian.

Michael didn't know how short his priestly career would be, nor the lasting impact of those mere thirteen years on the Catholic Church in America.

From a young age, Michael had stood out as student. The "excellent deportment and proficiency in his studies"[10] noted by his teachers got him promoted so many times he finished his basic education at age thirteen, a full three years ahead of the normal schedule. He was already thinking about the priesthood as a young teen, but he first went to work with his father at the brass factory in their hometown of Waterbury, Connecticut, to help support his younger siblings, seven of whom would live past infancy. The McGivneys were a typical Irish immigrant family—devoutly Catholic and working class. Like so many others, Patrick and Mary had left the poverty and hunger of Ireland with no more skills than an expertise in rather backward potato farming. They were from the same town in Ireland and both of their families settled in Waterbury, where others from their village had already made a home. Patrick picked up metal molding, allowing him to get a better job than many in the factories all over the East Coast. He was even able to squeeze out

---

[10] Douglas Brinkley and Julie M. Fenster, *Parish Priest: Father Michael McGivney and American Catholicism* (New York: William Morrow, 2006), 24.

the several hundred dollars a year it took for Michael to pursue seminary studies.

Then he died suddenly in 1873, casting a shadow not only over the family but also over Michael's vocation. Michael left St. Mary's College in mid-course, knowing he would never return. He had to take care of his mother and siblings. The McGivneys were luckier than many working-class families who lost a breadwinner, though. Michael's two sisters just younger than him were already working, and the older of the two was about to marry. With the two women and the new brother-in-law pitching in, they could keep the family and home together even without help from their older brother. Michael, though, couldn't support himself through seminary. That's when the bishop stepped in.

At St. Mary's Seminary, Michael was noted for his organization, calm, piety, sense of humor, and enthusiasm for baseball. As for his thoughts of becoming an erudite Jesuit, he had decided that his was the "arena of stirring toilers rather than that of placid thinkers,"[11] as a priest who had known him put it. From the Sulpicians who ran St. Mary's Seminary, he had learned that academic learning was valuable, but his main concern as a priest would be for souls themselves. He was ordained by Bishop Gibbon in the Baltimore cathedral on December 22, 1877.

His first assignment was assistant to the ill, aging pastor of St. Mary's in New Haven, Connecticut. The parish with its newly built stone church encompassed the neighborhood around Yale University. Its touches of gothic grandeur and its location in the shadow of a premier American university represented the struggle of its parishioners, mostly immigrants, to make a place for themselves in American society. Shortly after the church

---

[11] Brinkley and Fenster, *Parish Priest*, 54.

was finished, the neighbors complained that their aristocratic neighborhood had been blighted by a Catholic monument. The half-empty coffers and pews behind the grand facade also reflected the precariousness of the material success of these upper working-class families and the sad truth that most men stopped attending church around age twenty. They were either too busy getting ahead or simply preferred other amusements to Sunday Mass and church organizations, but in the worst-case scenario they fell into alcoholism. It wasn't easy being a Catholic immigrant, or even the son or grandson of one, in America.

With his parishioners' aspirations and struggles in mind, the young priest launched into his ministry. He gave catechism classes to the children, revived the Total Abstinence and Literary Society for the young adults, visited the elderly, and acted as chaplain for the local jail. He soon found himself running the day-to-day aspects of the parish, too, when the pastor left the city to escape the unusually hot and dangerous summer.

"I have not had time for even one day's vacation since I left,"[12] he wrote to one of his former professors.

Not that anyone would have thought he minded. On the contrary, everyone thought that they were Fr. McGivney's special ministry. The old ladies and children loved him, the young men flocked to him, and the ambitious respected him. At the pulpit, his voice, his perfect diction, and his clear sermons captivated his congregation. A blind beggar who wasn't even Catholic attended Mass every Sunday just to hear "that voice."[13] His unassuming gentility, calm strength, and childlike joy inspired trust and confidence everywhere he went.

---

[12] Brinkley and Fenster, *Parish Priest*, 75.
[13] Brinkley and Fenster, *Parish Priest*, 64.

He also had a way with souls and was instrumental in several prominent conversions. The two most talked about were the conversions of Alida Harwood and James "Chip" Smith. Miss Harwood was the daughter of a distinguished Episcopalian minister in the neighborhood. She had started attending St. Mary's to listen to Fr. McGivney's sermons. When she was dying of malaria at just twenty-five, she asked for Fr. McGivney and received the sacraments of the Church. James Smith's conversion attracted the attention of the local newspapers. This young man was convicted of killing a police chief and was awaiting his execution at the local jail. He responded to Fr. McGivney's spiritual counsel enthusiastically, and the priest helped him prepare for his death. Five days before the execution, Fr. McGivney celebrated a High Mass for him in the jail and then delivered a message from the prisoner to the community.

"I am requested by Mr. Smith to ask pardon for all faults he may have had and all offenses he may have committed, and at his request I ask for the prayers of all of you, that when next Friday comes he may die a holy death,"[14] Fr. McGivney said, swallowing back tears.

The priest was there, too, on the day of execution.

"To me this duty comes with almost a crushing weight. If I could consistently with my duty be far away from here next Friday, I should escape perhaps the most trying ordeal of my life, but this sad duty is placed my way by providence and must be fulfilled,"[15] he told the reporter from the local newspaper covering the hanging.

---

[14] Brinkley and Fenster, *Parish Priest*, 136.
[15] Brinkley and Fenster, *Parish Priest*, 136.

Fr. McGivney helped many families through the loss of a loved one. Death from disease or dangerous working conditions could steal a family member away at the most unexpected time. When the deceased was the breadwinner, Fr. McGivney followed the family especially closely, as he did the Downeses.

Edward Downes, Sr. was the son an Irish immigrant who had worked his way up from selling newspapers on street corners to owning his own news dealership and reading room, a good business in an aristocratic university town and the greatest success an Irishman could hope for in that era. He had expanded his father's business and the family fortune through investing. The Downeses were considered the most prominent and wealthy family in the parish. But a downturn in the market in 1873 had almost ruined them. Edward lost his business and his investments. But he kept going. The family, increasingly numerous, moved into a small house, and Edward opened a new, if much smaller, news shop. He was rebuilding his fortune, awaiting the birth of his fourteenth child, and putting his eldest son, Edward Downes Jr., through seminary. Then he died of "brain fever"[16] in December 1881. He had left no savings or assets other than the functioning news counter and family home. Like Fr. McGivney had done, Edward Jr. left his studies to see to the needs of his family.

The Downeses, though, were a much larger family to feed than the McGivneys had been, and the state of Connecticut wanted to make sure that the children wouldn't end up starving nor the teenagers running amuck. The probate court required proof the Mrs. Downes could provide for her children or they would be sent to orphanages or sent out to other families. At

[16] Brinkley and Fenster, *Parish Priest*, 8.

the first hearing, Edward Downes, Jr. had convinced the judge that even though he was just twenty-one, he could keep his father's business going and provide for his younger siblings. The judge was still concerned about the three next oldest Downeses, Alfred, nineteen; George, seventeen; and Joseph, fourteen. He wanted guardians appointed for them. The court required that a guardian not only be of good character and take full responsibility for the ward, but also put a bond set by the judge, in this case, 1,500 dollars for each boy. The Downeses' extended family had managed to come up with the bonds and guardians for George and Joseph, but no one could be found to be guardian for Alfred.

At the second court date, February 6, the judge accepted the guardianship arrangements presented for the two younger teenagers. Then he turned to Alfred. He asked him a series of questions and then asked if anyone present was willing to step up as guardian for him. Fr. McGivney stood up. He told the judge that he didn't have the required money, but he did have the pledge of a retired grocer named Patrick McKiernan to act as surety. If Fr. McGivney failed in his guardianship, the grocer would pay the "penal sum"[17] of 1,500 dollars. The judge accepted the arrangement.

That evening, he also had a meeting with the most respected men of the parish that he hoped would help prevent situations like the Downes's in the future. He gathered them together in the church basement to propose an idea that he had been working on for months: a distinctly Catholic fraternal benefit society. Mutual aid societies were popular and generally served two purposes. They gave members a social group to belong to and functioned

[17] Brinkley and Fenster, *Parish Priest*, 11.

as a kind of member-owned-and-operated insurance program in the event of illness or death. For a family like the Downeses, such an association would have prevented the scramble to keep the family together and afloat after the death of the breadwinner, but most mutual aid societies were secret societies that smacked of freemasonry and had underlying aims at odds with the Catholic Faith. Nevertheless, the sense of belonging that they offered attracted many Catholics who were often excluded from trade unions and other common organizations. There were already other Catholic fraternal societies such as the Catholic Order of Foresters and the Ancient Order of Hiberians, but Fr. McGivney thought that they lacked the vibrancy to compete with the appeal of secret societies. He wanted to start something that would be more than a life insurance company or an ethnically based Old World transplant. He envisioned a mutual benefit society both Catholic and American in identity, able to form its members into the American Catholic gentlemen they aspired to be and do good in wider society. This was the grand idea that solidified that night into the Order of the Knights of Columbus. The motto Fr. McGivney gave them was "Charity and Unity." (A third item, "Fraternity," was later added.)

The initial members named Fr. McGivney their founder and wanted to elect him president. Fr. McGivney, though, only accepted only the position of secretary. As a pastor he had other duties to attend to, and if the organization were to last, he knew it had to be led by the lay members themselves. In March, the Knights of Columbus were officially incorporated. Fr. McGivney sent out a letter to all the pastors in Connecticut inviting them to form councils at their parishes.

"[Our primary object] is to prevent people from entering Secret Societies, by offering the same, if not better, advantages to our members. Secondly, to unite the men of our Faith throughout the diocese of Hartford, that we may thereby gain strength to aid each other in time of sickness; to provide for decent burial, and to render pecuniary assistance to the families of deceased members," he explained.[18]

Councils grew slowly in the first years. The order was competing with the Catholic Order of Foresters and was little understood as an organization. But as it gained its footing, Fr. McGivney resigned as secretary. He was meant to serve them as a priest, he told the men, and remained chaplain. In 1884, he got a new assignment from the bishop, pastor of St. Thomas Church in the factory town of Thomaston. His final Mass at St. Mary's was a teary goodbye between congregation and priest.

"Never, it seemed, was a congregation so affected by the parting address of a clergyman as the great audience which filled St. Mary's yesterday," the *New Haven Evening Register* reported. "There was never a more energetic or hardworking young priest stationed in New Haven than he."[19]

At his new parish, Fr. McGivney continued to promote and defend the order. Some Catholics suspected that it was just another secret society. One such questioner was a fellow priest who wrote anonymously to the *Connecticut Catholic* with such accusations. Fr. McGivney replied:

The Order of the Knights of Columbus is the same now as when first instituted. viz.: It is an Order composed of Catholics and instituted for the welfare of Catholic families.... Not only in sickness, but when death takes

[18] Brinkley and Fenster, *Parish Priest*, 109.
[19] Brinkley and Fenster, *Parish Priest*, 174.

the support of the family away, the Knights of Columbus comes to the relief of the widow and the orphan in a very substantial manner.... The constitution and by-laws of the Knights of Columbus contain nothing collusive to the rules of the Church. Although but a few years organized, the Order has effected incalculable good in many households.[20]

In fact, the Knights of Columbus had paid out their first death benefit shortly before. From 1885 on, the order grew exponentially. As he had at St. Mary's, Fr. McGivney also poured himself out in his new parish.

In 1890, he developed a serious case of pneumonia. Remedies for consumption and his iron will not withstanding, he slowly declined until his death on August 14. He was only thirty-eight years old.

This time, he left behind not only a weeping congregation but also six thousand members of the Order of the Knights of Columbus, a legacy that would only continue to grow.

Today that legacy is miraculous. Fr. McGivney was declared venerable in 2008, and in May 2020, a miracle through his intercession was approved. In 2014, Michelle Schachle was expecting her thirteenth child when doctors told her and her husband, Daniel, that their unborn son not only had Down syndrome but also fetal hydrops, a rare and fatal condition where fluid builds up around the vital organs of an unborn child. According to neonatal specialists, there was no hope for the baby's survival. He would die before birth. The family immediately turned in prayer to Fr. McGivney. They had long had a devotion to him,

---

[20] Brinkley and Fenster, *Parish Priest*, 181–182.

as Daniel worked for the Knights of Columbus and had been Grand Knight of his local council in Dickson, Tennessee, where the Schachles live. They went on a pilgrimage to Fátima with the Knights of Columbus, where they and others there prayed to Fr. McGivney for this intention. When they returned home, at the next ultrasound appointment, all symptoms and signs of fetal hydrops had disappeared. The attending doctor, a different physician than had given the Schachles the initial diagnosis, asked what they planned to name their son.

"His name his Michael," Michelle said through her tears of shock and joy.

Today Michael Schachle is a happy, active child, thanks to his patron Fr. Michael McGivney, and he attended his namesake's beatification in Connecticut in October 31, 2020.

∽

PRAYER FOR THE CANONIZATION OF
BLESSED MICHAEL McGIVNEY

God, our Father, protector of the poor and defender
of the widow and orphan, You called Your priest, Bl.
Michael McGivney, to be an apostle of Christian family
life and to lead the young to the generous service of their
neighbor. Through the example of his life and virtue, may
we follow Your Son, Jesus Christ, more closely, fulfilling
His commandment of charity and building up His Body
which is the Church. Let the inspiration of Your servant
prompt us to greater confidence in Your love so that we
may continue his work of caring for the needy and the
outcast. We humbly ask that You glorify Bl. Michael
McGivney on earth according to the design of Your holy

will. Through his intercession, grant the favor I now present: (make your request). Through Christ our Lord. Amen.

☞

Please report miracles and favors to:

Fr. McGivney Guild
1 Columbus Plaza
New Haven, CT 06510-3326
(203) 752-4000
fathermcgivney.org

Blessed Miriam Teresa Demjanovich
The Universal Call to Holiness

Born: March 26, 1901 (Bayonne, New Jersey)
Died: May 8, 1927 (Convent Station, New Jersey)
Venerated: May 10, 2012 (Pope Benedict XVI)
Beatified: October 4, 2014 (Pope Francis)
Feast Day: May 8

A revolutionary yet simple idea that we are all called to be saints—far preceding the universal call to holiness of Vatican II—remarkably came from a quiet New Jersey girl who went on to become a religious sister and was later elevated to being recognized as blessed on the path to canonization: "If people only sought God in all earnestness they would find Him And if all would only make use of the ordinary duties and trials of their state in the way God intended, they would all become saints."[21]

Bayonne

---

[21] Sr. Miriam Teresa to Fr. Benedict, O.S.B., August 19, 1926.

On March 26, 1901, Teresa Demjanovich was born in the city of Bayonne, New Jersey. Her parents Alexander and Johanna were hardworking and devout immigrants, in 1884 joining a flood of other young couples to form an enclave of Slovak families. Teresa was the youngest of five living children with two others having died as infants early in the marriage. Her siblings, Mary, John, Anna, and Charles recognized their baby sister for her goodness, remembering her as an obedient and quiet child, but they did not notice the depth of Teresa's spirituality. From the time she was about three years old, she was said to have had a mystical understanding of the meaning of the Trinity.

Her deeply religious family belonged to the Ruthenian Byzantine Catholic Church, St. John the Baptist in Bayonne. Teresa was baptized and confirmed in that rite when she was five days old. She attended religion class every day after school and made her first Holy Communion at that parish at the age of twelve. With her membership in two rites, Teresa's life can be seen as a bridge between the eastern Church and the western Church. Although her family was of the Ruthenian Byzantine Rite, she became a member of the Roman Rite. The Demjanovich family moved, and the children took part in St. Vincent Roman Catholic parish's social events, activities, and liturgies, with Teresa attending daily Mass there and experiencing a deepening of her spiritual life.

Her quiet and generous spirit came to the fore when her mother's health began gradually deteriorating. The family responsibilities as nurse and housekeeper fell squarely on Teresa's shoulders, and she accepted these duties cheerfully. Meanwhile, she attended and eventually graduated from Bayonne High School, where she finished second in her class. All of this time, Teresa had looked forward to a life as a contemplative religious. When school was finished, she wanted to enter the Carmelite Sisters, but they did not accept her application due to her significant vision impairment, which was incompatible with their principal activity of embroidering of vestments.

At her mother's dying wish, she enrolled at the College of St. Elizabeth, a school sponsored by the Sisters of Charity and the first Catholic college in New Jersey to award degrees to women. When she first arrived at college, it was a clash of cultures: she had been ensconced in an exclusively Slovak cultural environment since birth, but at the College of St. Elizabeth most of the students were Irish. At first, it was very difficult for her to accept the others and for them to accept her, but, gradually, they began to recognize her uniqueness and sought her out in times of difficulty. "If you need help, go to 'Treat'" became a common piece of advice, as she was known by that nickname. She was an exceptional student, exhibiting mastery of all her subjects and eventually graduating the college in May of 1932 *summa cum laude* (with highest honors.) In the Sisters of Charity archives maintained for her canonization efforts, a college term paper is saved with the professor's handwriting across the front of it, "I saved this paper because I believe that one day she would be declared a saint!"

She was well known in college for her religious piety, yet, despite her incredible spiritual and mystical depths, to her friends Treat was just a good, normal, capable young woman admired by her classmates. She was involved in everything: she was a member of the track team, participated in extracurricular activities such as Spanish Club, and was editor-in-chief of the college yearbook. She wrote poetry for the college anthology, performed in plays, and for fun enjoyed occasionally going to New York City for shopping, theater, and concerts.

During her college years, she would attend early Mass at the Convent's Holy Family Chapel and would spend free time between classes and extracurricular activities making visits to the Blessed Sacrament and prayerfully saying the Stations of the Cross as the Sisters did customarily. Her piety drew the attention of the General Superior, who inquired amongst the sisters about the identity of the girl displaying such devotion. Even before she became a Sister of Charity, she was known for her ardent prayer life.

While she waited for God to reveal His plan for her vocation, Teresa began working at St. Aloysius Academy in Jersey City, where she was an excellent teacher who maintained her calm and cheerful disposition despite her mischievous and difficult class of girls. When June came, she was happy to be relieved of her school duties and returned home to resume housekeeping work for her family. Her best friend at the college, who was a religious sister, advised her not to wait too long if she wanted to consider joining the Sisters of Charity. She encouraged Teresa on a visit after she graduated to make a novena before the feast of the Immaculate Conception, when the community customarily renewed their vows. When Teresa witnessed that display from the Sisters of Charity, she realized that she was called to be a member of that very congregation both for her own sanctification but also for the sanctification of the Sisters. She would later write to her spiritual director: "The immediate object is to help sanctify this community (The Sisters of Charity of St. Elizabeth) ... and all His spouses engaged in the active life (women and men religious) ... by bringing home to them by force of example and word that God desires with desire to become one spirit with them ... and this life of union, far from being incompatible with their state, is the one thing necessary, for upon it depends the fruitfulness of action."[22]

---

[22] Sr. Miriam Teresa to Fr. Benedict, O.S.B., August 19, 1926.

On February 2, 1925, Teresa's father died, and as a result, she did not enter religious life on that day as originally planned. Even though she was willing to begin that same day, the Sisters postponed her entry until February 11, the feast of Our Lady of Lourdes. She hugged and kissed her family goodbye and began her life as a Sister of Charity, embracing their charism of seeking to make the love of God known in the world through their works in the world in education, healthcare, and social services. For a Sister of Charity, charity was of course a very important virtue in the life of Teresa.

Sr. Miriam Teresa donned the novice habit and cap on March 17, 1925, and was given her religious name: "Miriam" after the Blessed Virgin Mary and "Teresa" after her baptismal patron and favorite saint, Teresa of Ávila. Sr. Miriam Teresa was an exemplary novice, as she devotedly kept all the rules and customs of the community, down to the smallest details. She prayed the required spiritual exercises and kept her housekeeping duties conscientiously.

Despite her aversion to teaching, she was assigned to the Academy of St. Elizabeth on the motherhouse grounds, where she faithfully fulfilled her teaching duties, which were in addition to all the charges throughout the convent like those of the other novices. Since it was a boarding school, Sr. Miriam Teresa ate in the refectory and slept in the girls' dormitory.

She spent a great deal of her private moments in prayer and was a true mystic. On at least a few occasions, she had what can only be described as supernatural experiences. Throughout the history of the Catholic Church, there have been over three hundred cases of saints and blesseds claiming visions of the Virgin Mary—most of these aren't officially Church-approved events or even investigated, but, because such apparitions are claimed by holy people, they are considered to have likely been authentic experiences recorded in hagiographies throughout history. Once she claimed that she saw a vision of the Virgin Mary while she was sitting in her college dorm room, where she would at night sometimes kneel and pray looking out to the campus. One night as she prayed, it became very light around where she was looking, and she witnessed the Blessed Virgin appear to her. One of her best college friends, Agatha Spinella (known as "Spin" to Teresa), came in to say goodnight and found her immobile and in a trance-like state. When asked if something was the matter, Teresa related that she had seen a vision of the Virgin Mary. The college has preserved that room with a plaque on the wall commemorating this event.

On another occasion, Sr. Miriam Teresa had a mystical experience with St. Thérèse of Lisieux. She had a great devotion to the Little Flower—Teresa's friends reported that when they went into her bedroom in college days, they'd always see two books left out on her desk: the autobiography of St. Thérèse and the Bible. One day in the late afternoon, Sr. Miriam Teresa—told by her mistress to go out and get some fresh air by taking a walk in the nearby wooded Nazareth Park—couldn't find another novice to accompany her as darkness approached, so she prayed to St. Thérèse of Lisieux, who had in recent years been canonized on the same day that Sr. Miriam Teresa had received her habit. She asked St. Thérèse to walk with her, and to her surprise the Little Flower mystically came in person to accompany her. Afterward, Sr. Miriam Teresa gave an account to Sr. Dolores, who said that the novice's face shone with a heavenly radiance when she spoke to her about it that evening.

When a new chaplain and confessor arrived, a Benedictine priest, Rev. Benedict Bradley, he quickly realized after hearing Sr. Miriam Teresa's confessions that he was advising a true mystic and a very holy person. Fr. Benedict admonished her not to share her secrets of her life about her intimate union with God with Sr. Mary Ellen, the Mistress of Novices who held a great deal of authority over the novices and alone determined whether or not they were allowed to make final vows. She was probing—as she should have been—about how Sr. Miriam Teresa was progressing.

A complicated situation with Sr. Mary Ellen arose when Fr. Benedict recruited Sr. Miriam Teresa for some assistance. One of his duties as chaplain was to give weekly spiritual conferences and, realizing Sr. Miriam Teresa's holiness, he asked the Mother Superior if the young novice could write a series of conferences for him. The challenge was that she was not to let anyone—even the Mistress of Novices—know that she was the author of his talks.

These conferences revealed how she lived out the mundane aspects of her day to day life under a vow of "greater perfection" with the promise to aim in her vocation for what was most perfect in thought, word, and deed. There was a certain irony in what she had developed: her set of writings is considered to be a masterpiece of theology and spirituality but was generated by a woman who only had a small amount of formal training in theology. She reflected on the purpose of her life in her writings: "As I understand it, God's purpose in my life is this in general: To teach all people that Our Lord's promise, 'All who love Me will keep My Word; and My Father will love them and We will come to them and make our abode with them,' is held out to every soul regardless of calling; and is the perfect realization of Jesus' prayer and ours: Thy kingdom come."[23]

---

[23] "Blessed Miriam Teresa Demjanovich (1901–1927)," Sisters of Charity of Saint Elizabeth, https://www.scnj.org/blessed-miriam-teresa.

Before she died, her confessor asked for her permission to take possession of her work. Her handwritten pages of conference notes were gathered and published as *A Greater Perfection* in 1928 as a book of twenty-six chapters of her conferences, and it has been translated into a dozen languages. Many requests came in wanting to know about the author, and she became known throughout the world. Her message of a universal call to holiness has endured, that God wants everyone to be a saint.

Her time as a Sister of Charity would be short-lived. Beginning around Christmastime in 1926, Teresa developed a throat problem, so she was sent to St. Joseph's Hospital in Paterson. Her condition was diagnosed as tonsillitis, and she was operated on. When she returned to the convent, the sisters noticed how weak she was. She was then sent in February or March to St. Elizabeth Hospital in Elizabeth, New Jersey. They finally determined that she had appendicitis and operated, but unfortunately it was too late: the appendix had burst, and she quickly died of peritonitis. Sr. Miriam Teresa Demjanovich entered eternal life on May 8, 1927 at the age of twenty-six, after only two years as a religious sister.

The Cause for Canonization

The cause for Bl. Miriam Teresa began almost upon her death as small leaflets were distributed with her picture and biography written by Sr. Mary Zita Geis, S.C., a contemporary of hers in the novitiate and the primary generator of the early devotion to Sr. Miriam Teresa. All of the local Catholic schools began to pray for her beatification and canonization.

Rome was petitioned to officially open an inquiry, and then Pope John Paul II gave his approval in June of 1980 that the cause of Sr. Miriam Teresa Demjanovich be introduced, allowing it to move forward with further examination of her life and awarding her the title servant of God.

On May 10, 2012, ten years after the submission to Rome of the *positio*, the nine hundred–plus page academic position paper attesting to her virtuous life, Pope Benedict XVI promulgated the decree establishing that Miriam Teresa Demjanovich had indeed lived a life of heroic virtue and would be designated as venerable. This set the stage for a possible future beatification and canonization.

In order for Sr. Miriam Teresa to be beatified, the cause needed to find one medical cure that was worked through her singular intercession. Boxes and boxes of petitions and reports of alleged miracles, favors, and blessings attributed to Sr. Miriam Teresa had been sent to the Miriam Teresa League through the years. In 1970, a woman had written a letter because in 1963 she believed that she had witnessed a true miracle. Unfortunately, when the letter was filed in the cabinet, it accidentally fell to the bottom of the drawer between two hanging folders.

When the letter was discovered twenty-seven years later, the miracle story that came to light involved the loss of eyesight of a young boy named Michael, the third of five children in the Mencer family living in Pennsylvania at the time and later in New Jersey. His mother, Barbara, recalled that most people just thought he was shy, but he in fact was keeping to himself because of his difficulties with his vision: he was suffering from headaches, walking into trees, and struggling to catch a baseball with his friends, as he only had reliable peripheral vision. When one day a motorist went to the family home to report that Michael had walked into a moving car, his mother took him to see Dr. Vincent Carter in Teaneck, New Jersey, who made the diagnosis of bilateral macular degeneration. His eyesight registered as 20/400.

The Sisters of Charity and the children at the school and the neighbors were praying to Sr. Miriam Teresa specifically for Michael that his eyesight might improve. His third grade teacher at the time was a nun who happened to be the director of the Miriam Teresa League, and one day she sent Michael home with a pamphlet and a round memento with a relic, a tiny hair of the saintly nun, to give to his mother. He walked home with it clutched in his hand and kept struggling to try to see it; but then suddenly everything changed:

> I was trying to look at it—trying to focus—with my peripheral vision but obviously I couldn't get details on it. I looked up and saw an orb but it didn't hurt my eyes—I thought it was the sun—but then when I looked back down ... and moved my finger over it I could see the hair in the memento! And it still didn't dawn on me that a miracle happened.[24]

His mother was cooking dinner and, when he came home and went up to her to explain that Sister had given their family the relic, she turned to him to see something astonishing:

> He was looking directly at me. His eyes were sparking and his face looked entirely different.... when handed that to me, I knew he was healed![25]

She took him back at Christmas time to see Dr. Carter, who could not explain the impossible change and simply smiled and

[24] "The Boy Who Was 'Cured,'" NBC News video, 1:57, October 1, 2014, https://www.nbcnews.com/video/the-boy-who-was-cured-336540739742.

[25] From interview with Barbara Mencer, "Miriam Teresa Demjanovich," *They Might Be Saints*, EWTN, 2019.

said, "somebody has been praying!" She told him about the Sisters and what happened with Michael.

The doctors at the renowned Wills Eye Institute, a famous ophthalmological center in Pennsylvania that treats the most severe cases, asked Michael's mother why she brought a child with twenty-twenty vision to the clinic. The cause medical expert wrote a summary to four doctors — two pediatric ophthalmologists and two general — and each of them reported after consultation with their colleagues, medical journals, and other sources that nowhere had they been able to find such a cure.

The report was sent to Rome, where it was examined by the Medical Commission of the Congregation for the Causes of Saints. Ultimately, nineteen doctors examined the medical record and unanimously declared the case to be medically unexplainable. After the commission of cardinals determined that it was an instance of singular intercession, the report was sent to Pope Francis, who declared on December 17, 2013, that this was truly a miracle, thus setting in motion her recognition as blessed on October 14, 2014, in New Jersey, the very first beatification in history on American soil.

<hr />

PRAYER FOR THE INTERCESSION OF
BLESSED MIRIAM TERESA DEMJANOVICH

Most Holy and Adorable Trinity, Father, Son, and Holy Spirit, for Your own glory and the sanctification of souls, glorify Your servant Bl. Miriam Teresa by granting to us the graces which we humbly ask through her intercession: (make your request). Amen.

Our Father, Hail Mary, Glory Be

They Might Be Saints

~

Please report miracles or favors to:

Sisters of Charity of Saint Elizabeth
P.O. Box 476
Convent Station, NJ 07961-0476
(973) 290-5315
scnj.org
mcanavan@scnj.org

Blessed Solanus Casey
The Friar of Humility and Consolation

Born: November 25, 1870 (Oak Grove, Wisconsin)
Died: July 31, 1957 (Detroit, Michigan)
Venerated: July 11, 1995 (Pope John Paul II)
Beatified: November 18, 2017 (Pope Francis)
Feast Day: July 30

Fr. Solanus Casey was walking through the Detroit hospital one day when he saw Art Ruledgee, one of the volunteers at the Capuchin Soup Kitchen, in the hallway on a gurney.

"Hey, Art, what's up?" Fr. Solanus stopped.

He had a tumor, he explained, and was on his way to surgery.

"Where is it?" the priest inquired.

Art pointed to his stomach, and Fr. Solanus laid his hand on the area for several seconds.

"Have the doctors give you a last check before they operate," he said and continued on his way.

Art asked his doctors to take one more look.

Detroit ★

They couldn't find the tumor anymore.

It's no wonder Fr. Solanus was the most sought-after priest in Detroit.

He was born Bernard Francis Casey on a farm in Wisconsin in 1870. His parents were Irish immigrants who headed west after the Civil War and bought a farm. "Barney" fell in the middle of the twelve-child Casey clan, nine of them boys. They were known as the Casey Nine, their own baseball team. Barney always played catcher without a glove or a mask. He refused to box with his brothers, though. He would not inflict pain on another person.

"Prayer, boys, prayer," Barney's father would round them up for the Rosary in the evenings. Barney had an inclination to the priesthood since he made his first Holy Communion, but further studies were out of the question at the moment. Instead, he and his siblings left home to find work to help support the family and make their own way in the world. As an older teen, he roamed Wisconsin and Minnesota working as a lumberjack, handyman, and prison warden. At seventeen, he found a part-time job as a warden at the Stillwater prison not too far from his parents' farm where the three Younger brothers, members of Jesse James's gang, were serving a life sentence. Barney, the soft-hearted warden, got into long conversations with the bank robbers, especially Cole. Such was their friendship that Cole gifted Barney a wooden trunk he had carved himself while in prison. Barney was still using it when he entered the Capuchins several years later, around the same time Cole was going through a conversion that would lead to his full pardon and release from prison.

At the age of twenty, Barney landed a job as a streetcar conductor in Milwaukee. Though he had remained faithful to the prayers and beliefs of his Catholic home, he seemed to have put thoughts of the priesthood aside. He enjoyed his job as a streetcar driver — he was one of the first in the country — and thought he may have found his life's work. He also fell in love and proposed marriage. She accepted, but her father's opposition broke up the engagement. Then one day after the breakup, driving his route as usual, he pulled the streetcar to a screeching stop and jumped down. A crowd was already forming around the man who had his girlfriend pinned down to the tracks and loomed over her with a bloody knife. Barney was deeply shaken. After his shift, Barney found a church and spent the night in prayer. He prayed for the couple and asked God what he could do with his life to prevent such sorrow and violence. He decided to become a priest.

The next year, he enrolled in the St. Francis High School Seminary in Milwaukee. He took to seminary life with ease. The challenge was the language. American seminaries at that time were mostly run by German priests who taught in German. Being Irish and never having learned German, Barney, naturally, struggled. After four years, he was asked to leave, and the rector suggested he enter a religious order instead. He went back home to Wisconsin and, following the advice of his spiritual director, wrote to the Jesuits, Franciscans, and Capuchins. He was accepted by all of them. Now what? He felt no strong call to any of them, so he asked his mother and sister to pray a novena with him leading up to the feast of the Immaculate Conception. At Mass on the last day of the novena, he heard a voice within him clearly say, "Go to Detroit." That was where the Capuchins, a strict branch of the Franciscans, had their novitiate. Barney wasn't excited. Their bushy beards disgusted him.

His reticence about his vocation disappeared the first night at the monastery. He showed up at the monastery late on Christmas

Eve of 1896, tired, delayed by three days of snowstorms. He went to his guest room and fell asleep until the sound of the bells and singing for midnight Mass woke him up, and he wandered down to the chapel. He would never forget the joy he felt at that Mass. If there were hints of Br. Solanus's holy future during his novitiate, his superiors didn't make a note of it. Br. Solanus, though, journaled all his life. As a novice, he admonished himself in his notebook, "Beware of congratulating thyself on the blessings wrought through thy medium."

After his first profession of vows, Br. Solanus again struggled in the seminary. He never managed to pull grades higher than "average" or "passing," despite his discipline and good will. His superiors started to question if had the intelligence required for the priesthood. His final vows were also approaching, too, his forever commitment to life as a Capuchin. Would he still want to be a monk even if he weren't allowed to be ordained a priest? At his superiors' request, Br. Solanus signed a statement saying he left his ordination completely up to them. For a young man who had been hoping to become a priest and had already dedicated years of study toward the goal, it was a profound act of humility and surrender to the will of God. In the end, his superiors decided he could be ordained but only as a "simplex" priest. He would not be allowed to give absolution or preach formal homilies. He was ordained in 1904 without making a word of protest.

His first assignment was Sacred Heart Monastery in Yonkers, New York, where the friars ran a parish. His superiors didn't quite know what to do with a priest like him. He was first given charge of the sacristy and the altar boys, jobs usually done by lay brothers. When a new superior took over, he switched Fr. Solanus to porter. Every morning, the priest was outside sweeping the front steps and sidewalk and chatting with the neighbors. Anyone who came to monastery, whether they had business with the superior or were looking for a handout, met Fr. Solanus first. People started calling him "the holy priest," and he became the friar people called on for especially difficult situations. One day, for example, he was asked to visit a woman who had just given birth and was fighting a life-threatening infection. He blessed her with holy water, and she started to recover.

Non-Catholics came to see him too. A nosy neighbor watched a rabbi go to the monastery every week. Apparently, the man had some kind of leg trouble, because he walked with a cane, until one day, he came out of the monastery without it. To those disposed, Fr. Solanus was always willing to present the evidence and arguments in favor of the Catholic Faith, but he never pressured. Religion, he wrote in his journal, is "the science of our happy relationship with God and our neighbors. There can be but one religion, though there may be a thousand different systems of religion." Conversion he left up to God.

After fourteen years in Yonkers, he was transferred to Our Lady of Sorrows, the Capuchin parish in Lower Manhattan, where he took up the duties of sacristan and director of the Women's Sodality. Compared to his last years in Yonkers, his time at this parish was like a retreat for him. With much more free time, he devoured books about everything from mysticism to the Church Fathers. He studied Scripture and spent extra time in prayer. Three years later, he was transferred to the monastery in Harlem and was again made doorkeeper. More and more frequently, people came to the monastery simply to see Fr. Solanus, to tell him their problems — marital problems, drinking problems, health problems, financial problems, family problems. He had a compassion and gentleness that made it easy to talk to him even about the most difficult personal matters. He seemed to intuit solutions to especially difficult problems. Sometimes he would look away into the distance for a moment. Then in a few gentle, softly said words, he would offer insight and advice, sometimes a prediction about the outcome. His visitors always left with a sense of peace. He also encouraged people to "thank God ahead of time" and "to do something to please the Dear Lord," an act of faith such as giving to the poor, returning to regular prayer, or enrolling in the Seraphic Mass Association.

He enrolled many people in the Seraphic Mass Association, a mission effort started by the Franciscans in Switzerland at the end of the nineteenth century. To become a member, you gave a donation, even a small one, and were then remembered as a member of the association in the prayers and Masses of the friars. The donations supported the foreign missions. In those days, it was common for people to come to the monastery and enroll when they had a specific need they wanted to put before God. But those enrolled by Fr. Solanus were coming back with stories of miraculous resolutions and healings at surprisingly large rates. In 1923, the provincial asked Fr. Solanus to start recording the reported favors. Over Fr. Solanus's lifetime, these extraordinary answers to prayer reached into the thousands and filled up seven notebooks.

In 1924, he was transferred to St. Bonaventure Monastery in Detroit and assigned to help the porter there, Br. Francis Sprick. It wasn't long before they just left the front door unlocked and put a sign on it, "Walk in." One day in 1925, Chevrolet employee John McKenna came in and asked Fr. Solanus to say Mass for his employer, which was on the brink of bankruptcy. Two days later, the car maker had an order for forty-five thousand cars and stayed head-to-head with its rival Ford for the next two decades. Hundreds of other visitors came to the monastery to talk to Fr. Solanus or ask for his prayers or blessing. His days could start as early as seven o'clock in the morning and last until ten o'clock at night, talking with drunks, the parents of a child disabled by polio, the blind, the deaf, young people discerning a vocation, the desperate on the brink of suicide—no matter how tired he was, no matter how many people were waiting, he never lost his patience and treated each person like he or she was the only person that mattered.

Luke Leonard, a real estate broker, took a seat in the hallway one day shaking from the side effects of his self-imposed alcohol detox. He had been wandering the streets all morning, not even steady enough to drink a soda. Fr. Solanus surveyed the hall and took Luke aside to a private room. Luke poured out his story to Fr. Solanus, his self-hatred, his struggles to stop drinking, his despair. A brother opened the door.

"Fr. Solanus, others are waiting," he urged. "Some are from out of town."

"Ask them to wait a little longer," Fr. Solanus said, still listening to Luke.

Finally, Luke ran out of words.

Fr. Solanus leaned in and asked him. "When did you get over your sickness?"

"You mean my drunk, Father?" Leonard asked, confused. At that time, no one usually considered alcoholism a disease.

Fr. Solanus laughed. Luke smiled, not embarrassed but encouraged. He left uplifted and never took another drink.

Though many confessed their sins to him, Fr. Solanus wasn't allowed to give absolution, so he had made an agreement with one of the other friars.

"Now go over to the church and I'll call Fr. Herman and he'll go over to hear your confession," he would say. "Now you told the whole story. Just give a résumé to Fr. Herman. He will understand that you talked to me and he'll give you absolution."

After forty years of consoling and advising, listening and blessing, his superiors sent him to retire to Huntington, Indiana, where the Capuchins had relocated their novitiate. The novices had heard about the "holy man" of the community and watched him like a hawk. They found him quirky, classically ascetic, warm, and authentically holy. One morning, a novice, terrified that he had a particle of host trapped in his beard, found Fr. Solanus in the sacristy. He whisked his hand through the novice's beard.

"Don't be scrupulous," he said, "It's probably just flint. If it's the host, the holy angels will take care of it."

He had a high, slightly squeaky voice from damage to his vocal chords caused by a childhood illness. He still played the violin badly with his self-taught skills from boyhood. He also played the harmonica for the bees in the orchard, though this was more successful. When they swarmed one afternoon, threatening to leave, it calmed them back into the hive. Always an advocate of the benefits of exercise, he did calisthenics in the garden. He ate very little in general, and at breakfast, he mixed everything from coffee to prune juice to cereal to toast together in one bowl. It couldn't have made anything taste better. He was thin, almost gaunt. Occasionally, someone saw him praying late at night in the chapel, motionless, or playing his violin before the Nativity scene, but they knew they had been privy to something Fr. Solanus had intended to be seen only by God.

During the last years of his life, Fr. Solanus suffered from a painful skin disease. Covered with skin eruptions, he was hospitalized in May 1957. He never complained. On the contrary, he said he was "offering (his) sufferings that all might be one." He wanted "the conversion of the whole world" and wouldn't have minded having more pain to offer up.

By July, he had worsened considerably, and by the end of the month, he was clearly dying. On July 30, his provincial superior and one of his biological brothers came to visit him.

"Tomorrow will be a beautiful day," he told them before they left.

They weren't sure what he meant. The next day, his brother thought Fr. Solanus actually looked a bit stronger. Without warning, he opened his eyes, reached his arms upward, and declared, "I give my soul to Jesus Christ." Then he died. He was declared venerable on July 11, 1995.

The miraculous cure of Paula Medina Zarate's ichthyosis, a genetic skin condition, occurred at St. Bonaventure Monastery in Detroit in 2012. It was the miracle identified and validated by Rome and led to his becoming the first American-born male (non-martyr) to be declared blessed. His beatification took place on November 18, 2017, at Ford Field in Detroit in front of an estimated crowd of sixty thousand people.

⌒

PRAYER FOR THE CANONIZATION OF BLESSED SOLANUS CASEY

O God, I adore You. I give myself to You. May I be the person You want me to be, and may Your will be done in my life today.

I thank You for the gifts You gave Fr. Solanus. If it is Your Will, bless us with the Canonization of Fr. Solanus so that others may imitate and carry on his love for all the poor and suffering of our world. As he joyfully accepted Your divine plans, I ask You, according to Your Will, to hear my prayer for (make your request) through Jesus Christ our Lord. Amen.

"Blessed be God in all His Designs."

Imprimatur: The Most Reverend Allen H. Vigneron, Archbishop of Detroit, May 2017

⌒

Please report miracles or favors to:

Cause of Blessed Solanus Casey
1780 Mount Elliott
Detroit, MI 48207
(313) 579-2100
https://solanuscasey.org/
solanuscause@thecapuchins.org

Blessed Stanley Rother, Martyr
The Shepherd Who Wouldn't Leave

Born: March 27, 1935 (Okarche, Oklahoma)
Died: July 28, 1981 (Santiago Atitlán, Guatemala)
Beatified: September 23, 2017 (Pope Francis)
Feast Day: July 28

His sister found Stan sitting alone in his bedroom staring out the window. But he wasn't really looking at the Oklahoma plain covered with just-cut wheat. His mind was some two thousand miles south hearing the water lap on the shores of Lake Atitlán and the children calling for Fr. A'plas. He wondered if they would even have a priest to celebrate Easter Mass for them.

"Stan," his sister said to him from the doorway.

"I have to go back," he turned to her and said.

It was true. She could see it in his eyes. His heart was in Guatemala. He knew the risks, but he couldn't let his

Okarche

fifteen years as a missionary end like this. He couldn't abandon his parish and the people his mission served.

Fr. Stanley Rother had pulled up to the Micatokla mission in Santiago de Atitlán, Guatemala in 1968 pulling a rock picker with his Bronco. He was the oldest of five siblings who grew up on the farm in Okarche, Oklahoma. In high school, he served as an altar boy and president of his school's chapter of the Future Farmers of America. When he told his parents that he wanted to become a priest, his father had asked him why he had spent so much time as a Future Farmer of America instead of taking Latin. It was a good question. As a seminarian, he did, in fact, struggle with Latin. To his credit, though, his subpar academic performance was likely from distractions of generosity. When something needed to be done around the seminary, whether it was plumbing or landscaping or mechanics or building mainte-nance, he volunteered. There was hardly a handyman job he couldn't handle, and he came to be relied upon. But he had to repeat his second year of philosophy studies, and when he failed several theology courses during his sixth year of seminary, he was asked to leave Assumption Seminary in Texas. A meeting with his bishop back in Oklahoma got him a Latin tutor and a second chance at Mount St. Mary's in Emmitsburg, Maryland. This time he was more careful about his extracurricular activities and turned to his fellow students, many of them whizzes at Latin, for extra help. Stan was "a real plugger," according to one of his classmates. What he lacked in natural talent for Latin he made up for with steady dedication. He also still kept his hands busy, too, leading the renovations of the seminary's famous grotto and starting a book bindery.

He was ordained in 1963 and assigned to St. Francis Church. His only priestly duty was to say Sunday Mass. He was really put there to turn an expanse of undeveloped acreage donated to the diocese into a retreat center. He spent most of his time clearing land and building cabins. He was an obvious choice for the job, but as he wrote to a friend, "I'm doing carpentry while others are doing priestly work." After finishing the retreat center, he did receive a couple of regular parish assignments as assistant priest. His parishioners respected him and his calm, kind demeanor, but other priests thought he lacked intellectual finesse and was too matter-of-fact. On some level, he felt a little dumb.

Meanwhile, the diocese of Oklahoma City was heeding the call of Pope John XXIII for missionaries in Latin America. Sponsored by the diocese, Fr. Ramon Carlin had left Oklahoma for Guatemala in 1964. He established a mission high in the mountains near the giant volcanic Lake Atitlán. It served the descendants of the Mayans whose way of life had changed little since the first missionaries had brought them Catholicism. Their mother tongue was Tz'utujil, not Spanish, which many only had a rudimentary grasp of, and they lived an agrarian life of subsistence and self-sufficiency. They ate the corn and beans they grew, clothed themselves with hand-woven wool garments, and got a little cash by selling their artisan goods to the tourists who came to see them and the lake. In modern economic terms, they were some of the poorest people of the western hemisphere. Half of their children died of malnutrition and disease before the age of five.

Guatemala was headed for turbulent times too. The agro-export business dominated the country. Most of the country's best farmland was controlled by a wealthy few who grew coffee and bananas for international markets. Guatemalans of European or mixed ancestry had long controlled coffee production, but at the end of the nineteenth century, foreign interests had started banana plantations. The largest of these was the United Fruit

Company, an American holding that owned hundreds of thousands of acres and also had a monopoly on the transport system. People of indigenous descent, who accounted for almost half of the population, and poor *ladinos*, people of mixed ancestry, either worked for the large landowners with few protections or eked out a subsistence living on small plots of land. In 1944, a revolution had led to elections and democratic reforms in the country — universal suffrage, the legalization of labor unions, free press, and social security programs.

The next president, Jacobo Arbenz, went a step further and inaugurated land reforms. He expropriated with compensation large tracts of private, uncultivated land and challenged the United Fruit Company's monopoly on transportation. United Fruit lost a third of its land holdings. There was an active communist party in the country, but it was politically marginal, and Arbenz was not a communist. Nevertheless, the U.S. State Department justified military intervention to topple Arbenz as part of the anti-communist crusade of the post-war era. Supported by the United States, a string of governments brought to power by rigged elections followed the ten years of Guatemala's democratic spring. All democratic reforms were reversed. Over the next three decades, the agro-export industry would also triple its million-dollar profits while increasingly encroaching on lands used by indigenous people. In 1960, a small group of the military balked and went rogue, initiating a thirty-six-year conflict called the "Guatemalan Civil War." In reality, the various groups opposing the government with arms were never very numerous enough to justify the tens of thousands of people killed by the Guatemalan government.

But when Fr. Rother arrived at the mission in 1968, the conflict had not yet reached the highlands of Santiago Atitlán. "This peace is a comfort to us who live in a world beset by unrest—political, social, and religious. Happily this is not so evident here in Guatemala," he wrote back home to Oklahoma. Santiago Atitlán had a population of about twenty thousand people, and the mission also served the surrounding villages.

Besides Fr. Carlin, there were other priests, three nuns, a nurse, and two papal volunteers at work there. Fr. Carlin had started a weaver's cooperative, a farm, a radio station for educational purposes, a credit union, and a small clinic. He was also working with locals to create a written form of Tz'utujil. Most evenings after dinner, the conversation turned into a discussion on how to approach mission work—should they try to impose modern norms, or should they immerse themselves in the local culture and work for change over the long term? Fr. Rother usually excused himself and went to his room to listen to music, his way of relaxing after a long day. The discussion didn't interest him. He simply didn't think in those terms. His approach to mission work was simply to do what he thought needed to be done to help the people in front of him.

Fr. Carlin first sent Fr. Rother for an intensive Spanish course. As with Latin, his progress was lackluster. The other missionaries decided Stan was a nice guy but doubted he would be able to contribute more to the mission than saying Mass. Fr. Carlin, however, saw that his plugger personality and practical skills would take him far. Undaunted by Stan's apparent difficulties with languages, he exposed the new missionary to the local language and also assigned him a parish. Fr. Rother blossomed. Now Fr. Francisco, as he went by his more Spanish-sounding middle name, he quickly started to pick up the local language, and he would be the only missionary to master it. The two priests also collaborated in building a small hospital in one of the mission villages. In 1973, Fr. Rother wrote home that he was preaching in the local language. His parishioners had dubbed him Fr. A'plas, Francisco in their native tongue.

As other missionaries moved in and out and Fr. Carlin retired, Fr. Rother remained. By 1975, he had become the pastor of the main parish in Santiago Atitlán and the *de facto* head of the mission. He experimented with new crops and built an irrigation system on the mission farm, brought in volunteer doctors, visited his parishioners in their homes, involved himself personally in their needs, and renovated the colonial church. The infant mortality rate dropped by thirty percent. He was also working with locals on a translation of the New Testament into Tz'utujil. When his sister Carolyn, now Sr. Marita, A.S.C., came to volunteer, she noticed how many babies were named Francisco.

As the mission progressed, so did the conflict in the country. In 1978, Lucas García became president. During his four-year term, more than thirteen thousand civilians would disappear or be killed. Any opposition, or potential opposition, was squashed, often with torture and bullets. He shocked the world when his military shot and killed a hundred civilians, indigenous who resisted being displaced from their land, and assaulted the Spanish Embassy, where student protestors and labor leaders had taken refuge. He then announced that the Church itself was behind the government opposition and vowed to rid the country of meddling catechists, priests, and nuns within two years. His main targets were Guatemalans, but he also threatened missionaries. He started in the lowlands, where two bishops escaped death only by luck and a convent of missionary nuns got grenades thrown through their windows. As Stan watched, he knew the violence would eventually come higher.

Wearied by work and worry, he went back to the States for a few weeks to rest and pray at his alma mater in Maryland, where his old classmate Fr. Harry Flynn was now rector. Later archbishop of St. Paul-Minneapolis, Fr. Flynn never forgot their conversations. Stan described the injustices against the indigenous peoples and the need he felt to speak out but also the danger he knew he incurred. Back in Guatemala, his next report to the diocese described the exploitation of the poor by the agro-export industry. Stan never involved himself in political questions, though. He was unassuming, non-confrontational, low-profile, and practical. But neither as pastor nor preacher could he ignore grave injustice. By now, he didn't have to speak out; simply being a pastor to the poor put him in opposition to the regime. In May, he wrote back to Oklahoma in a hand-delivered letter:

> An anonymous hate sheet ... made its debut a few days ago. The school director, teachers, anybody of importance in town made the list. I was number 8 ... Guatemala is systematically doing away with all liberals and even moderates in the government, and labor leaders, and apparently there are lots of kidnappings that never make it into the paper.... The president wants to expel all those religious who were catechizing the people.
>
> The reality is we are in danger ... All classes and group meetings have been canceled. We are working in smaller groups. My associate and myself are seen less in the street and almost never leave the rectory at night. The tactic of the government has been to kidnap those they think are leaders, torture them and kill them ... If I get a direct threat or am told to leave, I will go. But if it is my destiny that I should give my life here then so be it ... I don't want

to desert these people and that is what will be said, even after all these years.[26]

In October 1980, the military set up camp on part of the mission farm and stole its crops. Stan said nothing. He didn't want conflict, and it would have been futile, or worse, anyway. As Stan explained in another letter, the government claimed they were there to protect the village from the guerillas, but there were no guerillas in those areas, and definitely none threatening the town. A small group had passed through in June and drawn a little attention by making promises to the people, but they hadn't been heard from since. Within four days of the military presence, five Ateticos disappeared, one of them the director of the radio station the missionaries had established and a friend of Fr. Stan.

"Anyone who has made an advancement at all is being pursued," Stan wrote to his bishop, "I still don't want to abandon my flock when the wolves are making random attacks. A nice compliment was given me recently when a supposed leader in the Church and town was complaining that 'Father is defending the people.'"

Stan put fences and locks around the church and the rectory. Hundreds of villagers slept in the church at night while catechists kept watch. Stan slept in a different room of the rectory every night, and often with his shoes on, prepared to run, if necessary. At the beginning of January, a lead catechist named Diego Quic was kidnapped right in front of the rectory, where he was going to sleep for the night for safety. Fr. Stan heard him yelling for help and went outside, but all he could do was watch three

---

[26] Donna Whitson Brett and Edward Tracy Brett, *Murdered in Central America: The Stories of Eleven U.S. Missionaries* (Ossining, NY: Orbis Books, 1988), 107–109.

masked men take him to a van. He described to his bishop in detail what had happened.

"Then I realized, Fr. Pedro, Frankie Williams and I had just witnessed a kidnapping of someone we had gotten to know and love and were unable to do anything about it. They covered his mouth but I can still hear his muffled screams for help," he wrote his bishop.

> As I got back to the rectory, I got a cramp in my back from the anger I felt that this friend had been taken off to be tortured for a day or two and then brutally murdered for wanting a better life and more justice for his pueblo.... He was 30 years old, left a wife and two boys, ages 3 and one.... I am not ready to call it quits, yet ... we don't know if Diego's presence here with us will affect us directly.... Just say a prayer on occasion that we will be safe and will be able to be of service to these people of God.... The shepherd cannot run at the first sign of danger. Pray for us that we may be a sign of the love of Christ for our people, that our presence among them will fortify them to endure these sufferings in preparation for the coming of the Kingdom.

Stan drove around the fields outside for days hoping to at least find Diego's body. Four days after Diego's disappearance, seventeen civilians were killed at a coffee plantation nearby in retaliation for a guerilla attack. Fr. Stan went to see the bodies and bring the Catholics to the church for burial. This, too, could have exposed him to the anger of the government. By the end of January, over thirty people had been kidnapped in Santiago Atitlán. He wrote to the diocese asking for donations to help support the widows and orphans left alone in the wake of the violence. He asked that the donations be deposited discreetly. His charity could be construed by the government as seditious.

On January 12, Stan was in a nearby village. The two other American missionaries there warned him that they had heard about a plot to kidnap him. One of the priests snuck Stan and his associate, the newly ordained Guatemalan, Fr. Pedro Bocelo, out of the highlands rolled up in blankets in the back of a truck. They hid in Guatemala City for a couple of weeks while Stan arranged a visa for Fr. Pedro. He wouldn't leave the country without him. Back in Oklahoma, Stan helped around his family's house and farm and at nearby parishes. Ronald Reagan took over the White House for his first term as president and ramped up the anti-communist rhetoric surrounding American policy in Latin America. In March, Stan was asked by a friend to preach at his parish in suburban Oklahoma City. He took the opportunity to explain the truth of the situation in Guatemala versus the message of the government. A couple weeks later, a letter arrived at the offices of both the archbishop and the Guatemalan Embassy. In it, a parishioner who had been at that Mass warned the authorities that some parts of the church were involved in trying to establish a Marxist government in Guatemala. In Stan's case, nothing could be further from the truth.

In April, though, he got word from Guatemala that it was safe for him to return. He knew it was still risky, but he felt he had to go. While Fr. Pedro remained in hiding in Guatemala, Stan made it back to Santiago Atitlán in time to celebrate Holy Week. Things seemed to have calmed down, and for the next few months, life at the mission was cautiously normal. But this time, the death squads did a better job of keeping their plan a secret. Just after midnight on July 28, 1981, two men broke into the church and found Francisco Bocelo, a cousin of Fr. Pedro. The put a gun to his head and told him to lead them to Fr. Stan. "Father, they've come for you," he yelled as they got close to the door. Fr. Stan was ready. He opened the door and put up a fight. "Kill me here," he shouted and fought as hard as he could. The attackers finally pinned him in a corner and shot him twice in the head.

He was officially declared a martyr, which paved the way for him on September 23, 2017, in Oklahoma City, to become the first American-born male in history to be beatified.

⁂

PRAYER FOR THE INTERCESSION OF BLESSED STANLEY ROTHER

O faithful shepherd, Bl. Stanley Rother, as priest and missionary, you tilled the soil with your hands and invited Christ Jesus to till the soil of your soul. You became a sign of love of Christ the Good Shepherd for your people and blessed their lives by your ministry. You stood firm and did not run from danger, bringing glory to God and His Church in your martyrdom.

Bl. Stanley, obtain from the Heart of Jesus (make your request), and pray for me, that I too may be a sign of Christ's love among His people. Teach me to faithfully till the soil of this life in the reality given to me by your Father, unafraid to stay with those God has given me, no matter the cost. Through Jesus Christ our Lord. Amen.

⁂

Please report miracles or favors to:

Catholic Archdiocese of Oklahoma City
P.O. Box 32180
Oklahoma City, OK 73123-0380
(405) 721-5651
stanleyrother.org

Blessed James Miller, Martyr

Wisconsin Farmer and Catholic Martyr

Born: September 21, 1944 (Stevens Point, Wisconsin)
Died: February 13, 1982 (Huehuetenango, Guatemala)
Beatified: December 7, 2019 (Pope Francis)
Feast Day: February 13

Br. James Miller was born near Stevens Point, Wisconsin. He was the oldest of five siblings in a Catholic farming family that he was always proud of. He loved farm work, but he started thinking about the priesthood as a high school student. His teachers, the Christian Brothers, convinced him that his vocation was as a teaching brother. In 1959, at the age of fifteen, he joined the Brothers' juniorate in Glencoe, Missouri. Essentially a high school for boys thinking of joining the religious congregation, the juniorate was also a self-sufficient farm that the boys helped to run. After finishing high school, he went on to the community's novitiate and was then sent to the University of Minnesota at Winona to study Spanish.

Br. James was not considered the most pious of the young brothers. He had a tendency to be late for prayers and wasn't the last to leave the chapel, either. But he had a remarkable generosity, simplicity, and friendliness that made him loved by all. He also had a deep faith in God, a sincere willingness to help others, and a laugh that could fill the whole monastery. He was human and easy to be with, a man who created union and harmony among his brothers. He had, they also said, the gift of gab. Even more than the topic of faith, James loved to talk about farming and recounted stories from his high school days in Missouri. He was good at farming too. He could drive a tractor with confidence, and there wasn't anything he couldn't build or fix. After earning a master's in Spanish, Br. James was sent to teach at Cretin High School in St. Paul, Minnesota. He taught English, Spanish, and religion, and he coached football. He also took on much of the building maintenance.

Somewhere along the way in his formation, James had caught the missionary spirit. He deeply desired to serve the poor in the missions. His superiors noted this when they admitted him to perpetual vows in 1969. Shortly after his final profession, one of the brothers at the mission in Bluefields, Nicaragua, got sick and had to return to the States. Br. James was sent to take his place. He took over the sixth-grade classroom at the mission school and was soon doing the building maintenance, too, of course. Then he taught in the high school, ran a bookstore, and started a soccer team. Whatever needed to be done, he did, quietly, willingly, and without needing to be thanked.

After four years in Bluefields, he was sent to Puerta Cabeza on the east coast of Nicaragua. Here he was named director of the school. The mission flourished under his leadership. He increased enrollment from three hundred to eight hundred students and enhanced the training the school offered. He built an industrial arts complex, offices, and a science building. He founded a volunteer fire department, training the firemen himself. He still took on the humbler tasks—teaching a full class schedule and doing building maintenance. He was often the one to sweep the floors and clean the bathroom, besides handling plumbing problems and building repairs. The Somoza government was impressed and contracted him to build ten rural schools.

Still, since Br. James had collaborated with the previous government to build schools, his superiors feared for him and recalled him to Minnesota. He obeyed with a heavy heart. It troubled him immensely to have to abandon the people he served. He promised them he would return. He was sent back to Cretin High School, teaching, opening lockers, and fixing toilets.

In 1981, he got his chance to return to the missions, though this time to Guatemala. But if Nicaragua could be considered life-threatening, Guatemala wasn't much better. In 1981, the country was in one of the most violent stages of a decades-long conflict. Br. James was appointed subdirector of the mission in Huehuetenango, Guatemala, where the brothers worked among the indigenous people, descendants of the Mayans, who were increasingly marginalized as their homes and farmland were taken over by commercial agricultural interests. The government military frequently tried to recruit the students who were supposed to be exempt. Each time the brothers heard that one of their boys had been picked up by the soldiers at the market or on the streets, they went to the military station and reclaimed him. Sometimes they had to insist, but the brothers wouldn't take no for an answer. Often, it was Br. James who went to rescue one of the boys.

"I am personally weary of violence, but I continue to feel a strong commitment to the suffering poor of Central America.... the Church is being persecuted because of its option for the poor. Aware of numerous dangers and difficulties, we continue working with faith and hope and trusting in God's Providence," he wrote to his sister a month before he died.

He knew he could be killed, and on February, 13, 1982, while he stood helpless and alone on a ladder fixing the school building, three men ran out from behind the church and shot at him at point blank range.

He was declared a martyr in 2018, catapulting him to the beatification stage of the canonization process. He was formally beatified at a Mass in Guatemala City on December 7, 2019. In order for him to be declared a saint, the cause for Br. James Miller is in search of one instantaneous, complete, and lasting healing miracle of a serious condition without any medical treatment resulting in the cure.

⤺

PRAYER FOR THE INTERCESSION OF
BLESSED BROTHER JAMES MILLER, F.S.C.

O Blessed Brother James Miller, you heard God's call to become a Brother of the Christian Schools and so became a sign of faith to youth in the United States and in Central America. You placed your life and your trust in Divine Providence and, for spreading the Faith, merited the crown of martyrdom. In a world that denies the dignity of the human person, obtain for us from Divine Providence an ever-increasing love of God and our neighbor, especially the poor and oppressed. Obtain for us also the favor we are now asking for (make your request) and the grace and strength to be a witness to Christ's love to all. Amen.

Imprimatur: +William Patrick Callahan, O.F.M. Conv., Bishop of La Crosse, February 7, 2020

☙

Please report miracles or favors to:

Christian Brothers of the Midwest
7650 S County Line Road, Suite B
Burr Ridge, IL 60527
(630) 323-3725
https://www.cbmidwest.org/

Chapter 5

American Venerables

Venerable Pierre Toussaint
Former Slave to Successful Businessman

Born: June 27, 1766 (Saint-Marc, Haiti)
Died: June 30, 1853 (New York, New York)
Venerated: December 17, 1996 (Pope John Paul II)

Pierre Toussaint's funeral filled St. Peter's Church on Barclay Street in Lower Manhattan that summer morning of 1853. High and low, black and white, French and English speaking, Catholic and Protestant came to honor perhaps New York's most beloved man. In the days that followed, tribute to him appeared in the city's newspapers and magazines. New Yorkers were still talking about him decades later.

"Why, Toussaint was a household name with us, and is still so," Emma Cary wrote in *Ave Maria* magazine late in the century. "People still talk of him today. He came everyday to our mother's house to dress my mother's hair, and our hair, too. My sister and I loved him and there was nothing I would not confide to

New York ★

him. It was like the confessional to talk to Toussaint, you were so sure of his secrecy. And no matter how freely we confided in him, he never swerved from his respectful demeanor. He always stood when he talked to us. 'Do sit down Toussaint,' someone would say to him. 'Madame I cannot,' he replied."

How many secrets of New York society he heroically took to the grave is easy to imagine. "Toussaint," he once told a client who had tried to elicit a bit of gossip from him, "is a hairdresser. He is no news journal."

He had become a hairdresser at about the age of twenty, while still enslaved by the Bérard family. The master and mistress had arrived in New York with their household of slaves and Madame Bérard's two sisters in 1797. They were wealthy plantation owners from the French colony St. Domingue, present-day Haiti. He gained entrée into the finest family—from French aristocrats to the Hamiltons—through the Bérard's connections, but then his personal qualities recommended themselves. He was not just an ideal hairdresser but the kind of person anyone would want to welcome into their home and call a friend.

Toussaint was at least the third generation of household slaves on the plantation. His grandmother, Zenóbie, ran the home, and her grandson's first position was playmate-servant to the master's children. He was also baptized, catechized, and taught to read and write in perfect French and to play the violin. He received the special attention of his little godmother, the Bérard's youngest child Aroura, just five years his senior (it was common at the time). Toussaint remembered these as the happy days of his childhood. The plantation was still prosperous when Pierre Bérard left it to his oldest son, Jean Jacque, and took the rest of the family to live in Paris on their massive accrued fortune.

But within a decade, the hundreds of thousands of blacks on the island were bucking the yoke of slavery. The Bérards and their plantation miraculously escaped the initial waves of violence. In 1797, Jean Jacque decided for safety's sake to take himself, his wife, Elisabeth Marie, and her two sisters to New York. He took along five servant slaves, among them teenaged Toussaint and his ten-year-old sister, Rosalie. He also packed enough money to support them all for a couple of years. By then, he hoped, French troops would have restored order.

Toussaint undoubtedly brought much to the Bérard household. He was intelligent, energetic, fun-loving, and endowed with genuine character. Whatever status or title he had in society, he was a person everyone wanted as a friend. To his clients, he offered more than a fine hairstyle.

In the Cary household, Emma wrote, "When we were little girls he would dance for us and show us how our parents had danced when they were young. He had taught himself many things. He had good taste and an excellent memory. He would quote Bossuet and Massillon — Massillon was his favorite author. If Toussaint had been an educated man he would have been illustrious, for he had a genius. But his great influence lay in his perfect Christian character, his exquisite charity and consideration for other, his tender compassion for all."

His compassion included anyone in need of help that he found in reach. Decades earlier, Toussaint and his wife, Juliette, had had to chuckle at the effect of their discreet charity. They had a white French neighbor who they knew was destitute. Without him realizing who his benefactors truly were, they regularly sent him portions of Juliette's cooking to ease his extreme poverty. When they met him in the street one day and asked how he was, he proudly spoke of the rich friends who had not forgotten him and sent him meals from their own table. They just smiled.

Initially, everything went as planned in New York. The Bérards were welcomed into the city's high society and had other French aristocratic refugees—both from Haiti and Old France—with whom to commiserate and hope. Toussaint quickly learned enough English to carry out the shopping, marketing (as it was called then), and other errands. In the evening, he pulled out his violin, played, danced, and mimicked Americans. The cold weather and the exile from family and home seemed less painful.

By the end of 1799, things in St. Domingue had gone from bad to worse. Jean Jacque decided he needed to return to the island to see if he could salvage something from the plantation. Before he left, he told Toussaint that he wanted him to learn hairdressing and had apprenticed him to Madame Bérard's hairdresser, Mr. Merchant. At the beginning of 1800, news came from St. Domingue. The colony was descending into deeper and deeper chaos, and while waiting for a ship to bring him back to New York, Jean Jacque had caught pleurisy and died. A few months later, the shipping company he had invested in went under. By this time, Toussaint was finishing his apprenticeship and starting to build his own reputation as a hairdresser.

The bills started coming in, but Marie Elisabeth Bérard had no means of paying them. She managed to hold most of her debtors off with promises, but there was one debt to a friend she considered a debt of honor. She called Toussaint and gave him her jewels with the mandate to sell them for the best price possible. Toussaint took the jewels but then went to his own purse and counted what he had. He calculated that with what he had saved from gifts and hair dressing tips, plus the money from his growing list of clients, it wouldn't take long to raise the needed forty dollars (today equivalent to hundreds of dollars). Several weeks later, he presented his mistress with two packages, one with the jewels and the other with the forty dollars. He soon learned of another debt. Toussaint's apprenticeship done, Mr. Merchant came to collect his fee, the equivalent of 750 dollars in today's values. Toussaint overheard the conversation and discreetly met his trainer outside. They negotiated a payment plan so that Toussaint could repay the debt over time.

Toussaint's hairdressing business was taking off. In New York at that time, it was common for wealthy women to have a hairdresser come to their home regularly, even daily, to fix their hair and their children's too. Toussaint also occasionally acted as valet for these families, as well as working out of his hairdressing shop. His days were long, and he had to move about the city on foot. Because he was black, he could not use the carriages and omnibuses available to the white public. He also had to watch his back. Blacks were always in danger of being harassed or attacked by jealous racists or the police of the day or, worse yet, of being kidnapped by "blackbirders" who would sell them to southern plantation owners.

What Toussaint thought, how he felt in the face of slavery and racist discrimination, and why he never became an abolitionist has not been left for history to know. Only two remarks have come down through the decades since his life. Abolitionists had, apparently, encouraged him to run away from Marie Elisabeth, perhaps after Jean Jacque had died, and it was obvious their fortune was lost. To the possibility, he said, "My freedom belongs to my mistress." Unjust as it was, Toussaint had a point: even if he ran away, only Madame Bérard could grant him his legal freedom. Black French in New York were also active in defending the few rights they had, even taking to the streets. When asked about his stance on abolition, Toussaint reportedly said, "You have never seen blood flow as I have." Nevertheless, he kept until his death an appeal from the French Free People of Color asking to make him an honorary member. Looking at his life, it seems he considered his mission to be undiscriminating charity and compassion done with a personal integrity free from servility.

This had started with his mistress, Marie Elisabeth, and her household. The mistress had remarried, but her husband was a disenfranchised Frenchman attempting to support himself as a musician. It was Toussaint's earnings that provided for the family. Marie Elisabeth continually promised to repay him, but Toussaint knew, of course, that it would be impossible. "I knew her full of life and gayety, richly dressed and entering into amusements with animation, and now the scene was so changed, and it was so sad to me. I had only asked to make her comfortable, and I bless God she never knew a want," Toussaint later reflected to a friend. Marie Elisabeth freed him shortly before she died in 1807.

His deep stores of compassion extended beyond his household and clients. From his twenties until his death in his seventies, his day started with the early morning Mass at St. Peter's Church. He joined the Blessed Sacrament Society and Benevolence Society too. He donated, raised funds, and visited the sick and poor. New York in the early 1800s had annual yellow fever epidemics. If they could, people fled the city for the country. Somehow, word had reached the parish of a lady sick and abandoned in the epicenter of the outbreak. Toussaint went to the empty Maiden Street and moved the barricades attempting to quarantine the area to find and tend to the poor lady.

In 1811, he bought the freedom of his sister Rosalie and his future wife, Juliette. Juliette was a fellow St. Dominguein whom he had met in his New York circle of black friends. When they married, he was twenty-nine and she was sixteen. Juliette was Toussaint's partner in his charitable works, and they loved each other deeply. They were never able to have children of their own, but they had one adopted daughter, Toussaint's niece. Rosalie's marriage had turned out badly, and her husband had left her with an infant and tuberculosis. The baby, christened Euphémie by Toussaint, was weak too. Toussaint lavished his little niece with attention and walks in the fresh air, certain that she would recover. He had to bury his sister, but his niece became the apple of his eye. Around this time, Toussaint also heard the last news about his mother and grandmother in St. Domingue. The colony had descended into complete disorganization and violence, and he never heard from them again, though he never stopped looking for them.

Toussaint had lost all connection with his loved ones from his childhood in St. Domingue when in 1822 he met by chance a French woman who knew his godmother, Aroura Bérard. The Bérards, he learned, had lost everything in the French Revolution, and Aroura had had to resort to running a tobacco shop to get by. She wrote to Toussaint, rekindling the childhood affection.

The reconnection also made Toussaint think of moving to France. He was actually a French citizen, not an American, since he was born in a French colony. He also had other friends in France, former clients who had returned after the violence had ended. In France, he would have a freedom he would never enjoy in America. His friends, however, advised against it. He would never have the business success there that he enjoyed in New York. Hairdressers simply weren't called on as often in Paris, and he would have to work years to get into the high-paying circles.

If he wanted to live in France, he would need to be able to live independently. For years, Toussaint planned—and then canceled his plan—to move his family to France.

At the end of 1829, Toussaint suffered another loss. Tuberculosis had come back for Euphémie, a mere fourteen years old. Toussaint thanked God that she had passed away without a painful struggle and that she would know the goodness of God in Heaven. Still, he grieved deeply. He lost weight and refused to see his friends, but he never stopped attending Mass. Slowly, with the help of prayer and Juliette and other friends, he accepted it as God's will.

Thirty years into his career, Toussaint had become a wealthy man, between his and Juliette's hard work (she ran a boarding house) and their investments. A friend asked him, "Toussaint, why do you work so hard, you are the richest man I know?"

"Madam," he replied, "I have enough for myself, but if I stop working, I will not have enough for others."

Then, in 1835, Toussaint had his fortune, and the hope of moving to France, wiped away. In December of that year, the Great Fire, as it came to be called, burned thousands and thousands of city blocks. Almost all of Toussaint's investments—real estate and fire insurance—were lost. It's estimated that he lost 95 percent of his net worth. His friends offered to take up a subscription for him, but he refused. Others, he said, needed the money more than he did.

No one knows how many individual requests for assistance of one kind or another he answered over the years. There was help for seminarians, for plantation owners like his mistress, friends and relatives in the Caribbean, and casual acquaintances down on their luck. People he didn't even know solicited him for help, and he gave what he was able to. He also got requests for advice, help finding a job, or to have some project looked after such as paperwork delivered or followed up on. He was creative in helping people find solutions and coming up with fundraising ideas. His major cause was orphans. He and Juliette offered their home to young black men with nowhere to go. They put up with the bad behavior that sometimes came with their difficult backgrounds and helped them get settled in jobs and trades. Some apprenticed with Toussaint. He also donated to and fundraised for St. Elizabeth Ann Seton's new orphanage in New York, even though it only served white children. Through Juliette, they also had ties to the Oblate Sisters of Providence based in Baltimore, the first community of black religious, and supported their orphanage as well.

His fortune recovered with time with his never-ending hard work. In his mature years, his friends turned to him less for business but more and more for spiritual advice and prayers. "I have known many men and observed them closely. But I have never seen one that deserved as you do the name of a religious man. I have always followed your counsels, but now more than ever, for there are few like you," a friend from Port-au-Prince wrote him. Others later regretted not having written down his advice when he was alive.

Juliette passed away in 1851, making the last years of Toussaint's life lonely, though he kept attending daily Mass and doing charity work as long as he could get himself around the city. In his final decline, he never lost his genteel bearing or gratitude.

"Do you want anything?" a longtime friend asked him the day before he died on June 30, 1853.

"Nothing on earth," Toussaint said.

Pierre Toussaint's body has since been moved to the crypt of St. Patrick's Cathedral, and he was declared venerable in 1996.

They Might Be Saints

~

*Lord God, source of love and compassion, we praise and
honor You for the virtuous and charitable life of our brother
in Christ, Ven. Pierre Toussaint. Inspired by the example of
our Lord Jesus, Pierre worshipped You with love and served
Your people with generosity. He attended Mass daily and
responded to the practical and spiritual needs of friends and
strangers, of the rich and the poor, the sick and the homeless
of nineteenth-century New York. If it is Your will, let the
name of Ven. Pierre Toussaint be officially raised to the
rank of saint, so that the world may know this Haitian New
Yorker who refused to hate or be selfish but instead lived
to the full commandments of Heaven and the divine law
of love — love for God and for neighbor. By following his
example and asking for his prayers, may we, too, be counted
among the blessed in Heaven. We ask this through Christ
our Lord. Amen.*

~

Please report any miracles or favors to:

Pierre Toussaint Guild
1011 First Avenue, Seventh Floor
New York, NY 10022
(646) 794-2681
obmny.org
obm@archny.org

Venerable Henriette Delille
The Saint of New Orleans

Born: March 11, 1813 (New Orleans, LA)
Died: November 17, 1862 (New Orleans, LA)
Venerated: March 27, 2010 (Pope Benedict XVI)

In the 1830 census, Henriette Delille changed her identity. Though her mother, brother, and sister recorded their race as white, she told the census marshal that she was a free woman of color. In the answer to one question, she rejected the material, legal, and social advantages her complexion could have bestowed on her. Instead, she put herself in solidarity with her enslaved ancestors and other people of color she taught catechism to.

Her mother and her brother would scold her for it later, but she had other concerns. She had come to reject the plaçage system that had brought her mother and father together. She had always known she would never marry, but she now had a different reason.

New Orleans ★

They Might Be Saints

Henriette grew up in the charmed world of the French Quarter of mid nineteenth-century New Orleans. Well, sort-of-charmed. She was charming, no doubt, at the quadroon balls held throughout the city. She had been raised to dazzle at these parties. Her mother had been taught French literature, dancing, and piano. But anyone who knew could see the crude reality under the elegance. None of the couples meeting each other would ever likely marry. It was illegal, as the ladies were of mixed race, even if just a fourth or even an eighth of their ethnic ancestry came from Africa, as was the case of Henriette. No matter their fair skin or their refined manners, they didn't have the pedigree the law required to marry the men there, who, by contrast, had completely Caucasian genes. Instead, the French and Creole men at the ball might offer these girls an informal contract as lovers, an arrangement many free women of color considered socially and financially superior to marriage with a black man, even one of mixed race like themselves. She would be his lover, and he would buy her a home and provide a regular income to support her and any children that may come along. They would never live together, and thus they evaded the laws prohibiting interracial marriage and cohabitation. The gentleman may or may not one day marry a white woman.

For Creoles like Henriette and her mother, their irregular situations did not preclude religion. New Orleans was a very Catholic city, and Henriette was very devout. The Ursulines had long run a school in the city for free women of color, which Henriette attended. When the Ursulines moved their convent to the outskirts of New Orleans, Sr. Marthe Frontier, a Dame Hospitalier from France, took over the education of these girls. She would be a decisive influence on Henriette. Sr. Marthe turned her most outstanding students into fellow missionaries, and Henriette and her close friends were among these privileged students. By seventeen, Henriette, Juliette Gaudin, a free woman of color from Cuba, and Josephine Charles were acting as godmothers for the baptisms of other colored people, including the enslaved. The three were also good friends. When Sr. Marthe left New Orleans in 1832, her students continued teaching and evangelizing in her spirit.

In 1834, Henriette was confirmed in the Cathedral of St. Louis. Only the most devout received this sacrament at that time in New Orleans. In the years that followed, Henriette, Juliette, and Josephine's names could be found in the sacramental records of New Orleans. They, along with other women, not only brought babies to the baptismal font but also acted as witnesses for marriages. They gave catechism classes to slaves and free people of color of all ages. They acted as visiting nurses for the sick and the poor too. Henriette received some opposition from her brother, Jean, since he feared her work compromised his own white identity that allowed him to move freely in society. Henriette only dug deeper into her vocation. She had come into a small inheritance in 1835 after her mother had had a nervous breakdown and was declared incompetent. She ensured that her mother was provided for and dedicated the rest of her small fortune to her works of charity.

Henriette wanted to completely dedicate herself to God, but religious life was closed to her as a woman of color. People of different races were not allowed to live under the same roof as equals. Still, she would find her vocation in religious life soon enough. With her lifelong friend and fellow missionary, Juliette, she began drawing up a rule to bring the women lay missionaries together in a more formal commitment. She called them the Congregation of the Sisters of the Presentation, and she described them as "a certain group of pious women founded for the purpose of nursing the sick, caring for the poor, and instructing the ignorant." In 1836, she, Juliette, and several other women privately dedicated themselves to personal holiness and service to others as Sisters of the Presentation. That year, Henriette wrote in one of her prayer books. "I believe in God. I hope in God. I love. I want to live and die for God."

In 1837, she met Fr. Etienne Rousselon, a newly arrived French priest appointed vicar of the diocese, chaplain of the Ursulines, and pastor of several parishes. In 1840, he would also found St. Augustine Parish, the first parish in the United States made up almost entirely of non-whites. He was enthusiastic about Henriette's community and took her and her sisters under his wing as their spiritual director. He also relied on them to help him in catechizing and educating at his parishes. By 1840, the Sisters of the Presentation had made such a reputation for themselves in New Orleans that the archbishop, Antoine Blanc, decided to apply for formal recognition for them as an association of the Sodality of the Blessed Virgin Mary in Rome, a centuries-old lay association founded by the Jesuits.

But Henriette wanted to go a step further. In 1842, Fr. Rousselon rented a house near St. Augustine's church where she, Juliette, and Josephine could live together and care for poor, elderly women. Instead, they first received an indigent man brought to them by one of the parish trustees. They couldn't refuse him. The house on Bernard Street became a new apostolate, and Henriette, Juliette, and Josephine moved to another house to where they could bring elderly women as planned. During the day, they divided their time between catechism classes for children, the women at the house on Bayou Street, and the indigent men on Bernard Street. The evenings and nights they reserved for catechism classes for slaves and free adults. Teaching slaves to read was illegal; even catechizing them without the permission of their owners was illegal. Nevertheless, Henriette and her sisters stealthily included basic education in her religion classes.

They were poor and shared what they had with the poor. They wore simple blue dresses and black bonnets. They took in boarders and did laundry to feed themselves and those they cared for. After paying the rent and taxes and ensuring those around them were fed and clothed, they often had nothing left over for themselves. Charitable ladies provided them with old shoes so they had something to wear in the garden when it rained. Their coats were like patchwork quilts. At dinner time, they often prayed for a donation, hoping some benefactor would send them leftovers from his table, even just a few teaspoons of sugar. Otherwise, after a long day, they would go to bed without eating. Sometimes, even when a donation came, they received nothing but cold hominy.

For a sort of novice mistress, they had Jeanne Marie Aliquot. The wealthy French immigrant had fallen into the Mississippi when she was walking off the boat that had just brought her to New Orleans and was rescued by a black man. From then on, she dedicated herself to the service of people of color. For several years, she had taken over the school for free women of color after Sr. Marthe left. She then continued teaching catechism. She had known Henriette for years. When she heard Henriette and her friends were starting a religious order, she offered to teach them.

In 1847, the Sisters of the Holy Family were incorporated as a religious charitable organization. This saved them from having to pay taxes and alleviated some of the financial pressure they felt. They were also able to fundraise to erect a new building for the men at Bernard Street. In 1851, Henriette used what was left of her inheritance to buy a house to create a permanent home for the growing religious family. Here she also opened a boarding school for girls.

But they still needed to make an official novitiate in a recognized convent. When a new order starts, the first members must go through a novitiate with an already existing community before making their initial religious vows and training future sisters in their own novitiate. This was more complicated for the Sisters of the Holy Family, since they were all women of color, and convents at that time were closed to them. Fr. Rousselon, nevertheless, convinced the archbishop to allow Henriette, Juliette, and Josephine to make a novitiate with the Religious of the Sacred Heart in 1852. They then made their first vows at the Church of St. Augustine.

The following year, a yellow fever epidemic engulfed New Orleans. None of the sisters fell victim to the disease, though they were deeply involved in caring for the sick. They suffered in other ways. Some of their students caught the illness, and the rest went home hoping to avoid getting it. With this, the sisters lost their income. "We came near to starving and could not get anyone to go and see about a donation," one of the first sisters, Sr. Mary Bernard Dreggs, recorded in a history of the community. Fr. Rousselon was in France, and their other usual benefactors were caught up in the epidemic. They turned to St. Leven. Their hands were still folded in prayer when they heard a knock on the door. On the porch was a barrel of rice and flour.

For the next ten years, Henriette continued her work for the poor. The Sisters of the Holy Family were beloved by those who knew them but had not gained wide recognition as a community of religious women. Instead of a habit, they still wore the simple blue dress. In numbers, they also continued to be small. At the time of Henriette's death in 1862, they numbered only twelve sisters, though they were still influential in expanding Catholic education and social services. Henriette died on November 16, 1862, after a long illness, probably tuberculosis.

Her obituary appeared in *Le Propagateur Catholique* on November 22.

> There died one of those women whose obscure and retired life had nothing remarkable in the eyes of the world, but is full of merit in the eyes of God. Miss Henriette Delille had, for long years, consecrated herself totally to God without reservation, to the instruction of the ignorant and principally to the slave.... Worn out by work, she died at the age of fifty years after a long and painful illness borne with the most edifying resignation. The crowd gathered at her funeral testified by its sorrow how keenly felt was the loss of her who for the love of Jesus Christ, made herself the humble servant of the slaves.

Curiously, in 2004, historian Fr. Cyprian Davis, O.S.B., found burial records that indicate that she gave birth to two sons between 1828 and 1833. Both died before the age of three. At the second burial, the priest noted that the mother couldn't afford the burial expenses and head stone and that the parish absorbed the expense. It could be that Henriette had entered into a plaçage relationship as a young teenager. In any case, the historical record leaves many gaps in her early years. Whatever may have been the situation of those children and their mother, history also shows that, without a doubt, Henriette demonstrated heroic virtue from the time of her Confirmation.

In holy irony, the Sisters of the Holy Family later purchased the old quadroon ballroom and turned it into a convent.

Henriette Delille was declared venerable in 2010.

They Might Be Saints

❧

Prayer for the Beatification of Venerable Henriette Delille

O good and gracious God, You called Henriette Delille
to give herself in service and in love to the slaves and the
sick, to the orphan and the aged, to the forgotten and
the despised. Grant that inspired by her life, we might be
renewed in heart and in mind. If it be Your will, may she
one day be raised to the honor of sainthood. By her prayers,
may we live in harmony and peace, through Jesus Christ,
Our Lord. Amen.

❧

Please report any miracles or favors to:

Sisters of the Holy Family
6901 Chef Menteur Blvd.
New Orleans, LA 70126
(504) 241-3088
HenrietteDelille.com
srdorisgoudeaux@verizon.net

Venerable Samuel Mazzuchelli

Missionary to the Early American Frontier

> Born: November 4, 1806 (Milan, Italy)
> Died: February 23, 1864 (Benton, Wisconsin)
> Venerated: July 6, 1993 (Pope John Paul II)

Br. Samuel Mazzuchelli was glad to leave New York City. The twenty-two-year-old Italian Dominican had grown up in the neighborhood around Milan's great cathedral and had seen Europe's most beautiful cities from Rome to Paris, but the New York of 1828, growing grand on the spoils of westward expansion and the labor of poor immigrants, had convinced him that material splendor and spiritual corruption went hand in hand. When he reached Philadelphia, though, his classically trained Italian vision couldn't help admiring the order of the well-planned city, and in Baltimore, the neo-classic architecture of the Cathedral of Mary Our Queen. This was the last of any real civilization he was to see for a while. His destination, Cincinnati, was a distant

Benton

eight hundred miles away, where fellow Dominican and diligent missionary Bishop Edward Fenwick looked forward to his arrival.

The two had met a couple of years before during Bishop Fenwick's recruitment tour of Rome. The American-born bishop of the diocese encompassing the old Northwest territory needed two things: money and, most of all, entrepreneurial, courageous priests willing to dive into that vast land without the comforts of civilization. Among all the Dominicans then studying for the priesthood, Bishop Fenwick had found only one, Samuel Mazzuchelli, the beloved youngest son of a well-positioned family of bankers, merchants, and politicians, ready to take on the challenge. At seventeen, he had renounced his inheritance and convinced his father to let him enter the Dominicans, but what Bishop Fenwick had said that turned him into a missionary wasn't left for posterity to know. In May 1828, Br. Mazzuchelli paid a final visit to his family and left for France with Fr. Frederic Rese, missionary and vicar of the Cincinnati diocese. After three months improving his French, Br. Mazzuchelli went on alone to Cincinnati while Fr. Rese finished his business in Europe.

Once across the Atlantic, the trip down the eastern seaboard made the young monk wish he already knew English. Since he had left New York, he hadn't found anyone who spoke either of the two languages he knew, French and Italian. With hand gestures and confusion and repeating "Cincinnati," he had managed to buy a ticket for the stagecoach west, but never in his life had he felt so embarrassed or isolated. The man waiting behind him in line at the ticket booth had noticed too. He approached Br. Mazzuchelli, took out his ledger book, and gestured. He understood that this stranger would take care of the talking, make sure he got to Cincinnati, and let him know the total of the expenses at the end of their travels. Br. Mazzuchelli took it as a lesson in trusting in divine providence and sat down in the stagecoach. Teetering and jolting from the speed, it passed families with Conestoga wagons, men with carts loaded to survive the winter, herds of sheep and pigs, and other stagecoaches racing each other to make the best time. Within Br. Mazzuchelli's lifetime, this flow of people along the National Road that stretched from the Potomac River over the Appalachian Mountains and then west to the Ohio River would fan out still further and turn his mission into the states of Michigan, Iowa, Wisconsin, and Illinois.

But when he reached Cincinnati that fall, the American frontier was still east of the Mississippi. After a brief stay in Cincinnati, Bishop Fenwick first sent the seminarian south to Bardstown, Kentucky, where the Dominicans had established their first American monastery, and then back north to Somerset, Ohio. Br. Mazzuchelli found the setting of the monastery in the woods dedicated to St. Joseph a perfect place to prepare for ordination. On September 5, 1830, he heard his name called out in the cathedral of Cincinnati and stepped up to the altar to become a priest. A month later, Bishop Fenwick sent him six hundred miles west to Mackinac Island in the strait joining Lakes Michigan and Huron. He caught a fur trader's boat heading that way. He had etched on a piece of paper a basic map of the two hundred thousand square miles entrusted to him. He was twenty-three years old.

At Mackinac Island, he initially noticed two things. First, St. Anne's Church served as gathering place and anchor for the practicing Catholics, who were glad to have a resident priest instead of having to await the infrequent visits of a priest from Detroit. Second, most of the five hundred people inhabiting Mackinac lived tough, poor lives as laborers for fur companies whose rich owners lived as gentlemen back east. Long estranged from the religious institutions by the lack of priests and resources in the wilderness, three generations had lost the peace and moral order religion brings with it. Few couples were married, and drunkenness and its accompanying moral ills were common. The islanders were largely French Canadian men coupled to Native American women, or the children of these unions. A smaller number of Chippewa, Menominee, and Ottawa had pitched their tents on the island and worked in the fur trade. There was also a smattering of businessmen, soldiers, and Presbyterian missionaries. In summer, the population swelled as fur trappers and traders met to collect and pay for the winter's worth of beaver pelts that then filled the warehouses of the fur companies.

Before winter closed in, Fr. Mazzuchelli also wanted to visit Green Bay across Lake Michigan. Again in a trader's boat, he traveled the three hundred miles south to the tiny town of scattered houses. There was no church, but he gathered the Catholics around a makeshift altar in the attic of a wood frame on the property of a welcoming parishioner. He also went out to the Menominee village. Fr. Mazzuchelli quickly realized that the Menominee people already believed in God, calling him the Great Spirit, and naturally understood and loved the Mass as similar to their own religious ceremonies. He explained the basics tenets of the Faith and told them to pray to the Great Spirit to help them know the truth. A handful of Menominee asked to be baptized. The memory and stories of the Jesuits who had passed through the area remained in the tribe, and he received permission to trade his Dominican white robes for the more recognizable cassock of a black robe. He also drew up the architectural plans for a church.

Back in Mackinac, he now encountered another characteristic of American culture in the hostility of the Presbyterian minister.

Word travels fast in a small town, and he learned that the Protestant minister was preaching with all vengeance against the Catholic Church in a series of fourteen lectures designed to convince everyone on the island of its evil. Fr. Mazzuchelli decided to confront the situation directly. He let his congregation know that he would attend all of the sermons of the Presbyterian minister and then address each point in his own discourse the following week in the evening, during which everyone was invited to ask questions or argue with him, including the Presbyterian minister. The charm of his thick Italian accent, the humor easily mixed in with the apologetics, and the goodwill shown in his smile and tone made his lectures popular. Although the Presbyterian minister never showed up, other curious Protestants did, and the controversy resulted in the conversion of several Protestants. In between, he visited the sick and dying near and far, blessed marriages, and heard confessions of traders and trappers who hadn't received a sacrament in as many decades as they had spent in the wilderness.

After the ice had melted, Fr. Mazzuchelli left for Green Bay again. Here, he started on his plan to build a church. Visiting each Catholic family, he asked them personally what they could contribute. Materials and funding secured, he drew up the architectural plans himself and then rolled up his sleeves to help move the rocks for the foundation and smooth the wood planks for the American frame house structure. He also spent time in the Menominee village, again. Visiting and teaching, he lived as one of them and accepted their ready hospitality—a piece of ground by the fire, a mat for a bed, and food in whatever quantity they had to offer. When he closed his eyes to prepare for Mass in a wigwam, he thought of the cathedral of Milan, but when he opened them again, he marveled at the sincere reverence of the

Menominee and the love of God, who didn't mind coming to this humble setting. To consolidate the emerging congregation, he also established a school, hiring a teacher who knew Menominee and some English and French with seed money from the government. Leaving the mission in the hands of zealous laypeople, he headed back to Mackinac for the summer rush.

He spent the next two years bringing the sacraments to three generations of French Canadian Catholics, and with the help of interpreters, preached and prepared catechetical texts for the Native American tribes. He visited the sick in far-off cabins, preached and catechized sometimes twice a day, and heard confessions for up to fourteen hours. Often lonely but never sad, he made the rounds of the settlements on Lake Michigan and beyond, from Mackinac up to Sault Ste. Marie, south to Green Bay, and then west to the Winnebago tribe and still further to Prairie du Chien. He reached the souls in that six hundred-mile range by boat or canoe, on horseback, on snowshoes, and over ice, snow, and mud. Sometimes he found himself so destitute he couldn't hire an interpreter. Another time, the journeys became so long and the provisions of nature so sparse, he had to eat a prairie rat. But even when in his simple house on Mackinac Island, he slept on the floor to keep prepared for the rougher conditions of travel.

In 1833, he returned to Detroit to have a prayer book in the Winnebago language printed. That year, the Diocese of Detroit had been carved out the diocese of Cincinnati and Fr. Frederic Rese appointed bishop. From Detroit, Fr. Mazzuchelli hoped to be able to visit his fellow Dominicans in Ohio and Kentucky, but Fr. Rese's pleas to keep him for the Detroit diocese won out. Back over Lake Huron he went, but this time with a Redemptorist priest to take over St. Anne's Church, allowing

Fr. Mazzuchelli to concentrate his ministry on the Menominee and Winnebago.

He made Green Bay his home base for the winter of 1833–1834, ministering to the French, Menomonee, and the Winnebago one hundred miles west. It proved the perfect opportunity to reach the Menominee who didn't come to church. The tribe used frozen Lake Michigan and Lake Winnebago for ice fishing and gathered there in more concentrated numbers than their spread-out summer camps. With an interpreter, he went around the lake discussing and arguing about the truths of Christianity around the fire of the wigwam. He encountered the sick and poor, sharing what he had. One evening, he fell asleep while his interpreter, Michael, engaged in an animated argument with their host. Fr. Mazzuchelli awoke to find that he had several new converts.

Encouraged by the Menominee chiefs and their desire to have him run the school the government had agreed to pay for as part of the most recent treaty, Fr. Mazzuchelli built a school in 1834. Besides providing an institution to support them in the Christian life, he wanted to teach them the best of European and American culture — agriculture and architecture for men, hand crafts for women, and history, reading, writing, and arithmetic for all, but in their own language. He hoped to integrate them into the country inevitably growing up around them without losing the best of their own culture.

Sadly, his plans for the Menominee school at Green Bay weren't working out. Although his proposal had already received approval, the Indian agent responsible for delivering the funds, future president Zachary Taylor, refused to support a Catholic mission run by an Italian. Instead, he gave the money to a Presbyterian mission that, in reality, served few Menominee. Fr.

Mazzuchelli wrote to President Andrew Jackson to advocate for the school, but he started to doubt that the government had any real intention of educating the Menominee and other tribes. The Winnebago tribe had also asked that their school be placed in Fr. Mazzuchelli's hands, but the money instead went to a Protestant mission, as well.

"It will be their fate," Fr. Mazzuchelli wrote in a memoir of his early mission life, "to continue in their wild, roving, and uncivilized state until the day when the civilized population of European origin will have filled the entire continent. Then the Indian will have left scarcely a trace of his existence in the land."[27] In fact, by the time Fr. Mazzuchelli wrote his memoirs of his first mission years in 1843, the missions that had been so successful among the Menominee and Winnebago had come to an end, as they had been removed yet further west. In the few years he had spent with them, though, he had baptized more than a thousand Native Americans. Even after obedience had sent him to other missions, he continued to advocate for them.

With the Redemptorists installed at Green Bay and Mackinac, Bishop Rese sent Fr. Mazzuchelli to Dubuque, Iowa. Miners were moving into what would become the Tri-State area where Iowa, Illinois, and Wisconsin meet, digging out lead to manufacture paint for the growing country. Farmers soon followed, but Fr. Mazzuchelli was still the only priest for hundreds of miles up and down and east and west of the Mississippi. He started in Dubuque like he always would, gathering the Catholics and building a church. They appointed Fr. Mazzuchelli architect and supervisor of the future church. He built to last, making St. Raphael's out

---

[27] Robert Trisco, ed., *Catholics in America, 1776–1976* (Washington, D.C.: National Conference of Catholic Bishops, 1976), 53.

of stone. Across the Mississippi, he was also building a church in Galena. As always, he also traveled, this time to the many mining settlements cropping up. The Irish miners renamed him Fr. Matthew Kelly, the best they could make of his Italian name, and it stuck. When Dubuque became a diocese a few years later and Bishop Loras choose his vicar, he named Fr. Matthew Kelly the second in command.

In his mission field, Fr. Mazzuchelli would make his most lasting contributions, founding thirty parishes and building approximately twenty churches. Civic leaders also called upon him. He led the opening prayer and gave an address at the first session of the Wisconsin Territory Legislature and designed public buildings and even cities, such as Iowa City and Shullsberg. In 1846, he founded a college for men in a log cabin in Sinsinawa. Within a few years, he had built a grand stone structure to house it. He also acted as president and taught, without neglecting the needs of the five widespread parishes in his care. In response to both the need for education and the interest of young women in joining the Dominicans, he founded the Sinsinawa Dominican Congregation of women in 1847. Then Fr. Mazzuchelli divested himself of his success for the freedom to do more mission work. In 1849, he turned the college over to the Dominican province and left for Benton, Wisconsin, where he would spend the next fifteen years.

Visiting a scattered flock, founding parishes, building churches, and starting schools continued to characterize his work. In 1852, the Dominicans asked him to resume the direction of the Sisters. Though the community initially struggled to grow, he and the few young women who persevered built Santa Clara Academy into one of the country's finest schools for women. With Fr. Mazzuchelli teaching many classes, it offered rhetoric, Italian, history, physics, astronomy, and many other subjects. The science lab was better equipped than some universities, and the young ladies debated topics such as voting rights for women and equality.

Still, his pastoral work drew him miles and miles beyond his rectory. On one late night sick call in the cold, he caught a severe case of pneumonia. The next day, the sisters found him immobilized by the pain in his chest and shoulder. For seven days he suffered, getting increasingly worse. When it became clear he was dying, he cried. "If you saw a person on a long painful journey, separated from his friends and house, and he found himself at the end of that journey, and got a glimpse of home, would you not allow him to rejoice?" he explained.[28] He died on February 23, 1864. In preparing his body for burial, the sisters found he had been wearing a penance chain long and hard enough for his skin to have grown around it. He is buried in Benton, Wisconsin and was declared venerable in 1993.

⁓

PRAYER FOR THE BEATIFICATION OF
VENERABLE SAMUEL MAZZUCHELLI

Lord Jesus, You called Your servant, Samuel, even in early youth, to leave home and all for a Dominican life of charity in preaching Your holy gospel. You gave him abundant graces of eucharistic love, devotion to Your holy Mother of Sorrows, and a consuming zeal for souls. Grant, we beseech You, that his fervent love and labors for You may become more widely known, to a fruitful increase of Your Mystical

[28] Sister Mary Nona McGreal, O.P., *Samuel Mazzuchelli, O.P.: A Kaleidoscope of Scenes from His Life* (Sinsinawa, WI: Mazzuchelli Guild, 1973), 56.

Body, to his exaltation and to our own constant growth in devoted love of You Who with the Father and the Holy Spirit live and reign one God, world without end. Amen.

⸚

Please report any miracles or favors to:

Dominican Sisters of Sinsinawa
585 County Road Z
Sinsinawa, WI 53824
(608) 748-4411
sinsinawa.org
communication@sinsinawa.org

Venerable Frederic Baraga, Bishop
The Snowshoe Priest

Born: June 29, 1797 (Mala Vas, Slovenia)
Died: January 19, 1868 (Marquette, Michigan)
Venerated: May 10, 2012 (Pope Benedict XVI)

"We will be saved," Fr. Frederic Baraga assured his native travel companion, Lewis. "Go straight on." The frightening sight of a rocky shore loomed ahead with the storm rising on the lake as they struggled in their canoe through the ever-higher waves. Fr. Baraga had prayed on through several hours of thrashing wind and rain. Soon, ahead, a small, calm river came into the clear. The travelers made it ashore and quickly erected a small cross of thanksgiving, a marker begetting the name "Cross River," as it is still known today. The journey was a forty-mile "short cut" across the open waters of Lake Superior from Sand Island to Grand Portage instead of the alternative route, which took a month and two hundred miles along the shore. Such adventures were not uncommon for the man who became known as the "Snowshoe Priest," and this was just one of many journeys to spread the Faith and bring the sacraments to his missions by snowshoe, like the one in February of 1845, when he made the six-hundred-mile round trip in five weeks of exhausting labors.

His exploits for evangelization were widely known in his native Slovenia, where Irenaeus Frederic Baraga was born on June 29, 1797, to a wealthy family in the castle Mala Vas near the village of Dobrnic in the Habsburg Monarchy, which today is part of the municipality of Trebnje. When he was very young, the family moved into an even larger castle. If he had wanted, he could have allowed his life to continue to be comfortable and easy. He always had his eye out for the less fortunate, with young Frederic being known to frequently give his shoes away to those children who had none. He started his studies at age nine and went away to a boarding school. He had a gift for languages, even far beyond the educational standard, which required students to demonstrate an ability to speak six languages at school; he became fluent in eight.

Frederic enjoyed travel and on summer vacations went on walking tours lasting weeks. In his visits to nearby countries, he experienced other cultures. Such physical activity and understanding of cultural differences prepared the way for his later years as a missionary.

Family tragedies hit Frederic when he was in his early years. When he was eleven years old, his mother died, causing him to turn to the Virgin Mary for consolation as his spiritual mother. His father then passed away four years later. With no living parents and as the brother to two sisters, he felt a strong responsibility to care for them. He himself had a guardian who encouraged him to go to law school, which he began at the age of nineteen in Vienna and later graduated from in two years in 1821. From his days at the university, he began to feel a call to something much greater that God was asking of him. He came under the influence of Clement Hofbauer, a Redemptorist priest and future saint who inspired Baraga to live a different kind of life offered as a gift to God, serving the poorest of God's children and bringing them the gospel. When the time came to further the canonization cause of the future saint, Baraga wrote in an 1865 letter to Pope Pius IX: "For three years I enjoyed the singular blessing of having as my confessor the Servant of God, a blessing I number among the greatest blessings Divine Providence has granted me during my entire life."

After petitioning the government and getting approval to enter the seminary, he was able to complete expedited studies, resulting in his ordination to the priesthood on September 21, 1823. While he was a priest in the diocese of Ljubljana, he wrote the first of seven prayer books for the faithful in the Slovenian language. His reputation for being a genuine and compassionate priest inspired many people to travel great distances to attend his Masses and have him hear their confessions. After just seven years as a priest, Baraga received some exciting news from the Leopoldine Society, an organization established in Vienna for the purpose of aiding Catholic missions in North America. He learned about a call from Bishop Edward Fenwick of Cincinnati to bring the Faith to the native people of the United States. Baraga signed up immediately and departed from France, taking thirty days to arrive in New York on December 31, 1830. He then made his way to Cincinnati, where he spent a short time with the bishop and worked among the German immigrants in the area.

He then embarked on his thirty-seven years of service as a missionary to the people of the Upper Great Lakes. Just eighteen months after he arrived in the United States, he built his first church, a small construction of logs and bark in Manistee, Michigan with the willing help of the natives. Fr. Baraga, from the very beginning, set out to preserve the culture and history of the native peoples in the Upper Peninsula, found in their language, dress, and tradition. He studied the Ottawa language under the instruction of the eighteen-year-old son of an Ottawa chief, who was attending the Cincinnati seminary. The next year he was sent to Arbre Croche, an Ottawa Indian mission, where he became fluent in the language. He would later publish *Otawa Anamie-Misinaigan*, the first book written in the Ottawa language, which included a catechism and prayer book. The catechism was popular amongst the native people, who used it to help them teach their own language, and it was an oft-requested burial accompaniment item as well. It was also useful as a faith teaching tool for the seventeen missionary priests — three of whom later became bishops — from Slovenia who followed in his footsteps to minister throughout the Great Lakes region and into Minnesota. Throughout his life, he would write twenty Native American books, including seven prayer books. His most notable contribution was his publication of "Grammar and Dictionary of the Chippewa Language" when he decided to travel north to minister to the Ojibway (Chippewa) Indians at La Pointe, Wisconsin on Madeline Island, at a former Jesuit mission on Lake Superior, where he remained for eight years.

In the early 1840s, Baraga was contacted by Chief Assinins and Chippewa Native Americans of the Keweenaw Bay, who were hoping to have a priest come to them to teach them the Catholic Faith. The chief himself was the first person to be baptized, laying the groundwork for other natives to be sacramentally welcomed into the Catholic Faith and helping to open the door to establish the mission there. In 1843, Baraga moved the mission to L'Anse, providing enough shelter with heat to help the natives avoid migrating south for the winter. He built thirty-three homes for the natives to live in as part of an effort to fight the movements within the government seeking to relocate the natives there to Oklahoma. He helped the natives secure food and lodging, for it was important to him that they had a homestead, a land of their own where they could grow their own food and live.

During the winter months, he famously traveled hundreds of miles each year on snowshoes during the harsh winters, thus earning him the nickname of the "Snowshoe Priest." With an approximate area of sixteen thousand square miles, the entire Upper Peninsula area of Michigan became the missionary territory of Fr. Baraga. In a diary entry from March 7, 1834, he reflected on the challenges of moving through the territory: "It is not easy for one to imagine how difficult a journey is through the primeval forests of North America where, like a swimmer, one must part the branches before himself in order to make a way through." Each trip proved difficult: "Fifteen miles from any house in the deep snow, an intensely cold night, no fire, completely exhausted! There was no choice but to walk on or to freeze."

He made those long and challenging journeys in very dangerous conditions by canoe and by snowshoe to reach new Christians, to bring them the sacraments, and to build chapels. If he was invited into somebody's home when he happened upon a homestead, he would sleep on the floor in front of the stove, with only a potato to eat for his meal. One winter, Fr. Baraga traveled from L'Anse to Copper Harbor, a distance of fifty-seven miles through an uninhabited region, with the singular mission to baptize a child, because he had heard that the child was in danger of death. For one five- to six-week trip from his famous

Keweenaw Bay mission, near L'Anse, he made the trek to the various native encampments, over four hundred miles round trip to Duluth, Minnesota on snowshoes in the middle of winter. During that time, he began the practice of rising at four o'clock in the morning in the winter (and then three o'clock in the morning in the summer) to start each day with three hours in prayer, a practice that he continued until the end of his life.

During this time, the population of European immigrants increased as they sought work in the copper and iron mines of the region, and he extended his ministry to them. Eventually, by necessity, he spoke in several languages at various times in the Upper Peninsula, with French Canadian families attending his Masses along with native people present there as well. He might deliver his homily three times in three in three different languages on any given Sunday.

The missionary activities of Bishop Baraga were widely known, but the clearest picture can be learned from letters to his sister, Amalia. In one letter dated June 10, 1831, Fr. Baraga wrote to her: "Happy day that placed me among the Indians, with whom I will now remain uninterruptedly to the last breath of my life." In time, Baraga became renowned for his work throughout Europe, as he sent further accounts in his own long, detailed, and frequent letters to Europe to places like the Leopoldine Society and the Society for the Propagation of the Faith, who published them widely as examples of its North American missions. Likewise, his three-volume diary, written starting in 1852 in several languages (primarily German, but also sections with English, French, Slovene, Chippewa, Latin, and Italian), preserved stories of his missionary travels and his relationship with his sister.

In the winter of 1853, Baraga learned of a family without medicine or provisions. He brought with him all that he could carry and embarked on a 250-mile trip to help them. With 90 miles remaining on the journey, his snowshoes gave out, and he was stuck in the snow. Baraga met a trader who gave him a pair of new snowshoes after he explained his situation. He was able to continue on his path, thanks to the kindness of the stranger. Perhaps he would have otherwise died on this trip without this intervention, but such fear never deterred him from making such a journey. No distance was too great for him to travel, no danger was too great for him to pass up a chance to help another and save a soul.

Later that year, Baraga was elevated by Pope Pius IX as the first bishop of the newly created Upper Peninsula of Michigan and its adjacent islands and was consecrated in Cincinnati on November 1, 1853, becoming the first bishop of the Diocese of Sault Ste. Marie, Michigan (now the Diocese of Marquette). The lack of priests and money were challenges he would face as bishop. His bishop's motto from Luke 10:42, found on his episcopal coat of arms, "Only one thing is necessary" (Latin: *Unum est necessarium*), is a clear reminder of his total reliance on God for everything.

In his sixtieth year, his stamina started to fail, but he still made midwinter trips to accommodate the needs of the native peoples. He continued to serve the dying in those who sought him for God's forgiveness in Confession. In the last decade of his life, his health gradually declined as he became intermittently deaf and suffered a series of strokes. In 1865, after twelve years at Sault Ste. Marie, Bishop Baraga moved the cathedral to Marquette to be near to the center of the area's population and activity and to be more accessible by ship and train. The Second Council of Baltimore in 1866 required his attendance as bishop. As he was getting ready to attend, he suffered a slight stroke and then had another severe one during the opening ceremonies.

He was very ill, but Baraga wanted to die amongst his people. He left the council quietly and without ceremony to travel back to Marquette. Baraga was very ill during his last months of life. At seventy years of age, his work was limited by illness, but he prayed and trusted up to the hour of his death.

He died on January 19, 1868, in Marquette, in the thirty-seventh year of his ministry to the native peoples of the Great Lakes. January 30, the day of his funeral, was declared a civic day of mourning in the city of Marquette, and all work was stopped in the city. In spite of the bitter cold and blizzard conditions, over three thousand people gathered at St. Peter Cathedral, which was filled to capacity and overflowing into the street with members of the Otchipwe tribe preceding the entrance of the clergy while strewing the way with evergreen branches. People from all walks of life gathered there that day who believed they had lived in the presence of a saint.

Baraga was declared venerable by Pope Benedict XVI on May 10, 2012.

⌒

Prayer for the Beatification of Venerable Frederic Baraga

O God, thank You for the life and holiness of Your servant, Frederic Baraga. I pray You will honor him by the title of saint. He dedicated himself completely to missionary activity to make You known, loved, and served by the people whom You love. As a man of peace and love, Baraga brought peace and love wherever he traveled. Lord, grant Ven. Bishop Baraga the grace of beatification. We ask this in Christ's name. Amen.

⌒

Please report any miracles or favors to:

Bishop Baraga Association
615 S. Fourth Street
Marquette, MI 49855
(906) 227-9117
BishopBaraga.org
BishopBaragaAssoc@gmail.com

Venerable Cornelia Connelly
An Unusual Path to Sainthood

> Born: January 15, 1809 (Philadelphia, Pennsylvania)
> Died: April 18, 1879 (St. Leonards-on-Sea, Sussex, England)
> Venerated: June 13, 1992 (Pope John Paul II)

Mother Cornelia Connelly was looking forward to the Christmas season with her three children. But they never came. Instead, the foundress and Mother General of the Society of the Holy Child Jesus received shocking news from the convent chaplain:

> I received a letter written to me by Mr. Connelly from France in which he says he has the children with him without giving any indication of where he is going, etc., and he orders me to forbid the Mother General, in his name, from having any communication with her children and does not wish to let her know the place to which he is taking them.

Philadelphia

Cornelia had not thought it would come to this. When she had contemplated all the sacrifices that God was asking of her, losing her children wasn't one of them. She had been willing to sacrifice the husband and family life she loved in order to let that husband become a Catholic priest, but she had never thought of abandoning her children. In their legal separation, she and Pierce had agreed that all decisions regarding the children would be made jointly. Now they had been taken from her by their father.

Then Cornelia Peacock, she had married Pierce Connelly in the Episcopalian church she attended in her hometown of Philadelphia. Cornelia was twenty-two, beautiful, intelligent, and exceptionally well-educated with a bold and spontaneous streak. Pierce was a recently ordained Episcopalian minister, handsome, intelligent, dramatic, and eloquent. They fell deeply in love and were, in many ways, well matched. They married on December 31, 1831, and shortly after the wedding, moved from Cornelia's hometown of Philadelphia across the country to Natchez, Mississippi, where Pierce had been appointed rector of the city's Episcopalian church. In those days, Natchez was a small town of some three thousand souls who mostly either owned or worked on cotton plantations. The couple gained the friendship of the best of Natchez society. Before their first wedding anniversary, Cornelia gave birth to their first child, Mercer, and her sister Mary came to live with them. The household also consisted of two slaves, who may have been given to them by the town's prominent doctor and their son's godfather. Cornelia taught them to read and later gave them their freedom. In 1833, Cornelia had their second child, Adeline.

Despite its success and the support he had in Cornelia, Pierce's work was wearing him out. Natchez had few Episcopalians, and his parish was spread out over the miles of cotton fields and wilderness surrounding Natchez. This was also a decade of intensely anti-Catholic nativism. Irish, Italian, and German immigrants were pouring into the country, changing the social composition of the almost exclusively Protestant nation and competing with other low-wage workers for jobs. In reaction, protectionist attacks on Catholicism itself circulated in pamphlets, preaching, and politics. Sometimes the rhetoric turned into outright violence against convents and churches. No one interested in religion or the affairs of the world could have ignored the anti-Catholicism in the air. The debate intrigued Pierce and Cornelia. At the same time, Pierce was becoming disillusioned with the Episcopalian church and was questioning Protestant claims of authority in general. Through his friends, Pierce met the perfect companion for his inquiring mind in the French explorer and ardent Catholic Joseph Nicollet. In their discussions in the Connellys' parlor, Pierce found himself agreeing more and more with Nicollet. In August 1835, he told his congregation he had resigned his position as rector to devote himself fully to studying Catholicism.

"I have perfect confidence in the piety, integrity and learning of my dear husband,"[29] Cornelia wrote to her sister Adeline. "I am proud to say that against all my prejudices and the horrors which I have nurtured for the Catholic faith I am ready at once to submit to whatever my loved husband believes to be the path of duty."[30]

She had followed the discussions with Nicollet and done her own studying, as well. Cornelia, too, had doubts about Protestantism, while her previous prejudices against Catholicism were

---

[29] Juliana Wadham, *The Case of Cornelia Connelly* (New York: Pantheon, 1957), 13.
[30] Wadham, *The Case of Cornelia Connelly*, 16.

falling away. Wherever duty and truth led, she wanted to follow wholeheartedly. As far their material needs were concerned, she trusted in God's providence. For the time being, they could live on the dividends of their investments.

Nicollet arranged a visit for Pierce with Bishop Rosati in St. Louis, where Pierce laid the question before him of becoming a Catholic priest. Cornelia later wrote to Adeline that it was not possible "if he desired it while I lived." Only if they separated could Pierce be accepted to the priesthood, a possibility Cornelia didn't seem to think Pierce would contemplate. Now, Pierce wanted to take his study of Catholicism and the chances of priesthood to the highest authority. In November 1835, the Connellys left Natchez for New Orleans to await a ship to Rome.

Shortly after their arrival in this city with deep French and Catholic roots, they were invited to attend the consecration of a new bishop. Afterwards, Cornelia decided she needed to be received into the Catholic Church before embarking on the voyage to Rome. Independently of Pierce and with his blessing, she started instructions. She was received into the Church on the feast of the Immaculate Conception. A priest present noticed the tears running down her cheeks when she received Holy Communion.

In Rome, Rosati's letter of recommendation served as entrée into high society. The English Catholic Lord Shrewsbury took the Connellys under his wing, and they soon met other American and English Catholics, including the Arundels and one of Mother Elizabeth Ann Seton's daughters. Pierce also got his audience with Pope Gregory XVI. The American almost-convert brought the conservative monk to tears with his story. The pope had a soft spot for cases like Pierce's. On March 16, Pierce requested to be admitted into the Church, confirmed, and considered for the priesthood. Cornelia sought advice from a young American priest, later the Archbishop of New York, Fr. John McCloskey, then studying in Rome.

"Is it necessary for Pierce to make this sacrifice and sacrifice me? I love my husband and my darling children. Why must give them up? I love my religion and why cannot we remain happy like the Earl of Shrewsbury and his family?" she asked.

Cornelia could have the assurance that, at least, any decision about the priesthood would take time. Pierce's desire would have to be tested, and she would have to give her consent for a separation. Though Pierce found sympathizers, he was also cautioned to move slowly. But whatever her misgivings about the future, Cornelia happily saw Pierce and the children received into the Church on Palm Sunday 1836.

Pierce enjoyed being the feted convert among people of prominence and power. With Lord Shrewsbury, he also went to England for several months to be part of the Oxford movement of converted Anglicans. For her part, Cornelia took music and painting lessons, learned Italian, improved her French, and explored the city with a deep interest in its history and architecture. She also received spiritual direction and visited the poor in Rome with the Earl of Shrewsbury's daughter. Her spiritual and natural joy coalesced. "I am cosmopolitan. The whole world is my country and heaven is my home," she wrote to her sister.

When Pierce returned from England, Cornelia conceived their third child. In 1837, disappointing news came from the United States. The markets that their investments were in were crashing. They were advised to return home. They took a leisurely trip through northern Europe and Vienna, where Cornelia gave birth to John Henry and Pierce delivered a letter to Cardinal Metternich, the most influential man in Europe at the time. In 1838, they were back in Natchez.

Through his brother, Pierce had found a job as a clerk, and Cornelia helped support the family by giving music lessons. They quickly renewed their old friendships, and even Pierce's old parishioners came to visit. Soon, another opportunity presented itself. Further west, the Jesuits and the Religious of the Sacred Heart, a congregation of women religious Cornelia had met in Rome, were starting a mission and schools. They needed an English teacher for the future St. Charles College. Would Pierce be willing? They couldn't offer a salary, but they could offer a house and education for the children. Cornelia could earn an income by teaching music lessons. In between the edge of the bayou and the American frontier, they set up their home in Gran Coteau, Louisiana, and started teaching. Pierce wrote to his brother that Cornelia was "happy as bird" in their new situation. The question of priesthood seemed to have gone latent. Amidst these pleasant times, the one dark cloud in the sky was the death of their newborn baby, Mary Magdalene, at seven weeks.

Over the Christmas holidays of 1839, both Pierce and Cornelia made a three-day retreat with the Jesuits. The days of prayer had left Cornelia more dedicated than ever to pursuing holiness as wife and mother in the backwater of Gran Coteau. Pierce, though, had become restless. In the silence of the retreat, he had pondered his discontent. He wasn't enjoying teaching English, and he found his students dull and the school poorly run. His family life was his only consolation, he wrote his brother. At the end of January, Cornelia wrote in her diary:

> Oh, my God, trim Thy vine, cut it to the quick, but in Thy great mercy root it not yet up. My God, help me in my great weakness. Help me serve Thee with new fervor.

A few days later, while watching her children play, a prayer left her heart almost without thinking:

> Lord if all this happiness is not for Thy glory and the good of my soul, take it from me. I make the sacrifice.

Two days later, in a freak accident, the beloved baby John Henry fell in a vat of boiling maple sugar. The burns were extensive, and nothing could be done. Cornelia held him for forty-three hours before he finally died.

By fall, she was several months along with her fifth pregnancy, but memories of Europe and notions of doing great things still floated through Pierce's head. After an eight-day retreat, on October 13, 1840, on their way home from Mass, he told Cornelia that he had discerned his vocation. He was meant to be a priest, and now. Had it not been for the grace of God, her broken heart would have fallen to pieces.

"This is a very grave matter," she told Pierce. "Think about it deeply and twice over; but if the good God asks the sacrifice, I am prepared to make it and with all my heart."

Cornelia agreed to live with her husband as brother and sister, and after Frank was born in March, Pierce got ready to leave for Rome. His excuse for returning to Europe was to take Mercer, now nine years old, to an English boarding school under the patronage of Lord Shrewsbury. Cornelia moved to the grounds of the Religious of the Sacred Heart with the two younger children.

While Pierce was in Europe, Cornelia had to figure out what new direction her life would take. She understood from other examples, such as Elizabeth Ann Seton, that her children could remain with her even if she chose to enter religious life. In September 1841, she made a retreat. "Examined vocation. Decided," she summed up in her diary. "Oh, my good Jesus, I will give myself to Thee to suffer and to die on the cross, poor as Thou wert poor, abandoned as Thou wert abandoned." At the end of 1843, Pierce called her to Rome. She had to give her consent to the separation personally before the pope.

Pierce applied for the priesthood in March 1844, and Pope Gregory XVI immediately accepted the request. The Connellys then finalized their separation, and Pierce began studies for the priesthood. Cornelia made a vow of perpetual chastity and went to live with the Religious of the Sacred Heart with Frank and Adeline. Pierce was allowed to visit Cornelia and the children frequently, and they exchanged letters freely. After only a year of preparation, the diocese of Rome admitted Pierce to the priesthood. In July 1845, he was ordained in the convent chapel. Adeline received her first Holy Communion, and Cornelia sang in the choir. Her smile and brightness surprised some guests and observers. Her joy, now, was having sacrificed her husband to God.

She had been accepted by the Religious of the Sacred Heart as a pre-postulant, but lived in a separate house on the convent grounds with Adeline and Frank. Adeline attended day school in Rome, and Frank would join Mercer at boarding school when he was older. Then Cornelia could begin her novitiate. For now, she followed the prayer life of the sisters and imposed enclosure on herself while raising her children.

Cornelia had initially thought her vocation lay in the contemplative life but in spiritual direction, she confessed she had a growing vision of a community that would "meet the wants of age" through all the works of mercy. Her spiritual director encouraged her, too, to think broadly. One day, watching Frank play, the name "Society of the Holy Child Jesus" came to her. Pope Gregory XVI then added his approval, telling her that she was not called to any existing congregation but to one not yet founded.

Under the direction of the American Jesuit Fr. John Grassi, she started to write a rule of life. She had thought to start small and perhaps in America, but circumstances led her to grander undertakings in England. Lord Shrewsbury and other aristocrats pointed out the lack of educational institutions for women, and the English Bishop Nicolas Wiseman offered Cornelia a convent in the industrial town of Derby. Cornelia arrived in England in October 1846, with Frank and Adeline and three young women who would become the first members of the Society. Pierce, too, was in England as chaplain to Lord Shrewsbury.

Under Bishop Wiseman's direction, Cornelia reluctantly sent Frank and Adeline to boarding schools to avoid criticism and misunderstanding. In England, Catholics were highly scrutinized and harshly criticized. The separation from her children was only to be for the duration of Cornelia's novitiate; nevertheless, it was salt in the wound caused by the breakup of her family. She would later say that the Society was founded on a broken heart.

"You see, I haven't given him to God for nothing," Cornelia had written to her brother-in-law about Pierce, but, as at other times, the new priest grew discontent. Also, though they were in relatively close proximity, he had been forbidden from visiting Cornelia personally. He started to resent his restricted access to Cornelia and the power of Bishop Wiseman to impose it. One day, in 1847, he surprised Cornelia with a visit. When she found him in the parlor, she quickly ended the encounter. Pierce responded with a scathing letter that brought her to tears. In response, she encouraged him to forget about the visit and also opened up about her own struggles. "You have not the violent temptations that I have, thinking of our little Bethlehem, nor have you perhaps gone through the struggles of a woman's heart. No, you never have," she wrote.

Besides having Pierce's molestations to deal with, Cornelia had inherited a heavy debt on the convent, and Bishop Wiseman's fundraising efforts were not as successful as he had hoped. Still, Cornelia persevered, and in just one year had started a day school for wealthier girls and night and Sunday schools for working-class girls. The community had also grown to twenty women. In December 1847, Cornelia took her religious vows and expected Pierce to bring the children to Derby. Instead, he used them to try to manipulate her.

As a woman at that time, she had little legal recourse to recover her children. Once again, she left everything in God's hands. Pierce, meanwhile, continued to try to regain control. He first posed as founder of the Society, presenting his own rule in Rome. After that failed, he made a complete about-face on Catholicism and sued Cornelia in English court for restitution of conjugal rights. He also dedicated himself to publishing anti-Catholic tracts. Though she eventually won the lawsuit, it all led to years of Cornelia being dragged through the press and subjected, along with the Society, to the judgments of Victorian Protestantism. Friends encouraged her to leave the country, but she stayed, knowing that a show of cowardice would do more harm than good and trusting in God instead. Eventually, Pierce settled in Florence with the children and left her alone. Her longing for her children, however, she carried to her grave. Mercer died of yellow fever in Mississippi at age twenty, completely estranged from her, and Frank and Adeline she saw again only as adults. By then, and perhaps because of Pierce's influence, it was impossible to restore intimacy. Still, Adeline later returned to Catholicism and dedicated herself to charity. Frank remained anti-Catholic, but nevertheless had his daughter educated by the Society. Cornelia prayed for Pierce her whole life and never spoke ill of him.

Perhaps Pierce had not counted the true cost of breaking up his family and becoming a priest or had not fully considered that by separating and taking priestly and religious vows, he and Cornelia had given each other to God over and above their obligations or claims as husband and wife. Cornelia fully realized this. "I am all God's," she wrote in her diary. One of the first postulants, who later became Cornelia's confidant, watched Cornelia endure lawsuits, betrayal, opposition, and calumny. Whatever inner turmoil and sadness she experienced, she remained calm, kind, and joyful. Through everything, and even as she aged, she retained a childlike joy and sense of humor. Many could feel the presence of God around her, and the sisters noted the brightness of her face when she received Holy Communion. Some claimed her prayers and even her touch brought healing and peace. Cornelia died in 1879 at the age of seventy-one and was declared venerable in 1992.

"We ought to look for a greater share of the Divine love in proportion as we are willing to sacrifice our natural happiness," she had written shortly after Pierce's ordination.

Her life is proof that this hope will be fulfilled.

⌒

PRAYER TO OBTAIN THE BEATIFICATION OF VENERABLE CORNELIA CONNELLY

O God, Who chose Cornelia Connelly to found the Society of the Holy Child Jesus, inspiring her to follow the path marked out by Your Divine Son, obedient from the crib to the Cross, let us share her faith, her obedience, and her unconditional trust in the power of Your love. Grant us the favor we now implore through her intercession (make your request) and be pleased to glorify, even on earth, Your faithful servant, through the same Christ our Lord. Amen.

☞

Please report any miracles or favors to:

Society of the Holy Child Jesus
Casa Cornelia
via Francesco Nullo 6
00152 Rome, Italy
shcj.org
Generalate@shcj.org

Venerable Augustus Tolton
America's First Black Priest

Born: April 1, 1854 (Ralls County, Missouri)
Died: July 9, 1897 (Chicago, Illinois)
Venerated: June 12, 2019 (Pope Francis)

Augustus Tolton was the first black, African American priest in the United States. The Healy brothers had been ordained before him, but despite their mother's slave status, they had had a white father who educated them and were able to move in society as white. Fr. Augustus Tolton, on the contrary, was the son of two slaves and had won his freedom first by flight and his priesthood by perseverance.

He often told the story of his escape from slavery with his mother and siblings when he was seven.

After the Civil War had broken out, his father had run away from the Hagar farm in Bush Creek, Missouri, to fight with the Union Army. After several months had passed, Augustus's mother decided she and the children couldn't wait for eventual

★ Chicago

victory. She had heard there were slave traders in the area and dreaded the family being separated. Downstream and across the Mississippi, the abolitionist town of Quincy, Illinois, beckoned to her, as it had to many others in similar circumstances. So one dark night, she wrapped up the toddler, handed Augustus and his brother Charles each a satchel of food, and then slipped out of their hut. They ran through the night in the direction of Hannibal. During the day, Martha disguised herself in plain sight as just another slave in the fields while the children slept. Then they ran again by moonlight with Augustus and Charles panting behind her while she carried their younger sister. Finally, they reached Hannibal on the Mississippi, a city split between Union and Confederate forces.

Martha tried to look nonchalant as she and the children went through town at dusk subtly in search of a way to cross the river, but some Confederate soldiers came around the corner and stopped them. They were about to be arrested, when two Union soldiers stepped in and asserted their control in that part of town. With their help, Martha found a rickety rowboat to cross the mighty Mississippi in. She had never rowed before. The soldiers pushed them away from shore, and her awkward strokes took the boat in a long, slow zigzag across the river. About halfway across, they heard shouts and gunshots. Bullets splattered in the water. The Confederate soldiers had seen them.

"Lay down," Martha Jane hissed at her crying children.

But it was too dark for the soldiers to hit their target.

Martha pulled and heaved her body weight against the oars and the water until she felt the boat scrape the Illinois riverbank and stop. She pulled little Anna out of the boat, and they all fell together in a heap on dry land.

"Thank the Lord, thank the Lord," she said, rocking her three crying children in her arms.

In the dark, they heard footsteps approaching. Martha's heart stopped. A group of men, both black and white, made a half circle behind them.

"We won't hurt you," said one holding a lantern. "We were passing by on our way to our shift at the wharf and heard the crying, that's all. You must be looking for Quincy, and you might be hungry."

They all opened their lunch sacks and offered what they had.

"Just follow the river north," their spokesman told Martha. "Quincy is about twenty miles off, but this here road leads right to it."

In Quincy, the Toltons found shelter with Mrs. Davis "for as long as they needed." The widowed woman had one daughter, Mary Ann, who was about Augustus's age and dying of tuberculosis. The arrangement turned out to be helpful for everyone. Martha quickly found work at the Harris Cigar Factory, and since Mrs. Davis worked the night shift as a charwoman in an office building, the mothers could alternate looking after the children, but Augustus and Charles soon joined their mother in making cigars. The Tolton-Davis household stayed together for years. Like the Toltons, Mrs. Davis was Catholic, and she introduced them to St. Boniface Church, the closest Catholic Church to the black section of town. It was the German parish, but for the cadre of blacks and others who didn't understand German, Fr. Schaeffermeyer repeated the Gospel in English, as well as a summary of the homily. Martha Jane and Mrs. Davis tried to be the first to enter the church and the last to leave to avoid crossing the white parishioners and having insults muttered at them. Fr. Schaeffermeyer had little understanding of his congregation's racial sentiments.

The first years in Quincy came with their hardships too. Charles, a year older than Augustus, died of pneumonia over the winter, and Martha Jane worried about her husband. The Civil War ended in 1865, and she held out hope that he was safe and would find them. After several months had passed, she inquired at the army office. Peter Tolton had died of dysentery in St. Louis early in the war. But life went on, and Martha had a deep faith. Sunday Mass was obligatory and prayer part of life. Augustus always said he had learned to pray and sing at his mother's knee. He also absorbed everything he heard at church. In the alleys of his neighborhood, he performed stories from the Gospel and acted out the Mass, often throwing in the German words he had picked up. His were lively, one-man productions of parables and miracles. He pulled now one, now another child onto stage to fill a momentary role or elicited a ringing "amen" from his audience.

The tobacco factory closed down in the winter, and when Augustus turned eleven, Martha Jane decided it was time for her son to go to school. She took him to St. Boniface's to see if he could attend there. Yes, of course, Augustus was welcome, Fr. Schaeffermeyer and the sisters who taught there assured. They did not anticipate the reaction to Augustus standing out amidst the previously all-white student body. The children tormented him until he broke down sobbing. Parents threatened to abandon both school and church and report Fr. Schaeffermeyer to the bishop. Sr. Chrysologus kept Augustus after class not only to tutor him but also to protect him from the children waiting for him outside. Fr. Schaeffermeyer stood his ground, but it was too much for Augustus. After a month, Martha decided it was best to pull her son out. Fr. Schaeffermeyer never forgot the sight when the two walked away: "After we drove them out, the mother's arms flung around her son."

The Toltons started attending the church across town, St. Peter's, and three years passed before Martha enrolled Augustus in school again. When he was fourteen, she sent him to the all-black public school. Here, too, Augustus became the object of bullying. He was lanky, darker than average, had no father, and still couldn't read. All these points his classmates turned into weapons of verbal abuse. Mary Ann Davis was also dying that winter. The pastor, Fr. McGirr, came to give her last rites and also met the Toltons personally for the first time. He chatted with Augustus and found out the boy was attending public school.

"You'll lose your faith there," the priest said. "Come to St. Peter's."

Fr. McGirr promised to take care of any objections. He and Martha agreed that Augustus would start in a month, and in the meantime, the priest would pave the way for him. On Sundays, his homilies reminded his parishioners of Jesus' words, "Let the children come to me," and "whoever puts a stumbling block before one these little ones, it would be better for him to have a millstone tied around his neck and be thrown into the sea." At school, the sisters prepared their classes to receive a black student with a combination of lessons and threats. Anyone caught insulting or otherwise being mean to Augustus in or out of school would receive the harshest punishments. At the rectory, Fr. McGirr simply refused to see anyone who came to complain about the situation. The strategy worked. Years later, Augustus said, "as long as I was at that school I was safe. Everyone was kind to me."

Sr. Sebastian also taught Augustus to serve Mass. From now on, his day started with Mass, either at St. Peter's, St. Boniface, or the convent. He then went off to either work or school. During the nine months that the cigar factory was open and he couldn't attend regular classes, Sr. Herline tutored him after his shift. He made his first communion at sixteen, a moment that made his heart exalt and want to be a priest. The more Fr. McGirr came to know Augustus, the more he saw a priest in him too.

Augustus was now eighteen and about to finish St. Peter's school.

"Augustus, would you like to be a priest?" Fr. McGirr asked the teenager one morning after Mass.

"Could I?" he answered.

"Of course," Fr. McGirr said.

He conferred with Fr. Schaeffermeyer. Despite the fiasco of Augustus's short time at his school, the German priest had taken a strong interest in the young man. He stopped and chatted with him or walked a few blocks with him when he saw Augustus coming home from the cigar factory. Now he pledged to see Augustus got a seminary education. The two priests decided the best plan was to propose to Augustus that he enter the Franciscans in nearby Teutopolis. Augustus was willing, but the Franciscans did not find him qualified. His odyssey to seminary had begun.

Fr. McGirr decided to write to their bishop in Alton about Augustus becoming a diocesan priest. "Find a seminary that will accept him and the diocese will assume the expenses," he charged Fr. McGirr. The priest wrote to every seminary in the country, but every single one replied in one way or another that they "were not ready to accept a Negro." In the midst of this, Fr. Schaeffermeyer entered the Franciscans himself. He left his replacement, Fr. Ostrop, a detailed debriefing, including instruction regarding Augustus:

> The sum indicated under "Education for a Priest" is intended for the Negro boy Augustus Tolton of St. Peter's Parish. Fr. McGirr of the Irish parish asked that I find a teacher who will prepare the young man for the

priesthood. The money is a private donation—not parish funds. I trust that you will do what you can for the Negro as he is indeed very worthy. I promised to help him and now request you to carry out my promise. I also ask that you take an interest in the boy so far as lies in your power.

Fr. Ostrop outlined a program of studies for Augustus and provided him with books until a teacher could be found. A few months later, he was given an assistant priest, Fr. Wegmann, who had a reputation as a scholar. With two other young men, both white, the priest formed an informal college at the rectory. This was Augustus's first seminary.

Fr. Ostrop had also heard of the recently founded St. Joseph Society for Foreign Missions, today called the Josephites. The small group of priests working in Baltimore among African Americans were an offshoot of the St. Joseph Society of Mill Hill based in England. He had Fr. Wegmann write to them about Augustus. They replied that they didn't have a seminary yet in America and so couldn't train Augustus for the priesthood, but they proposed three options: Augustus could come to Baltimore as a catechist; he could apply to the Mill Hill seminary in England, if he were willing to be a missionary in Borneo; or he could, at least for the time being, continue his studies in Quincy. More than willing to be a missionary, and thinking the surest possibility for the priesthood was in England, Augustus continued to study with Fr. Wegmann and save his pennies for an eventual journey across the Atlantic.

These were, at times, long and trying years. In 1875, Fr. Wegmann was transferred, leaving Augustus without a tutor. Fr. McGirr arranged to send him to a priest friend in Missouri, but that only lasted a few disastrous months, as the priest turned out to be a troubled drunk. Augustus returned to Quincy and then had a couple of strokes of good luck. He first found work as a saddle maker and then a good paying job at a bottling company. Fr. McGirr had also hired him as the parish janitor. When Augustus thought no one was around, he was heard singing while he cleaned. Augustus was also admitted to St. Francis Solanus University in Quincy.

He was now nearing the end of the learning Quincy could offer him. It had become more and more clear, though, that the Mill Hill Fathers in England didn't want to accept him and thought he should attend seminary in America, even though the Josephites still had no seminary. Fr. McGirr wrote to Bishop Baltes with a new plan. The Urban College in Rome trained men from all over the world to be missionary priests. Perhaps they would accept Augustus if Bishop Baltes went to them in person during his upcoming trip to the city. The bishop agreed. The answer, once again, though, was that Augustus should study in America. No one across the Atlantic could understand the obstacles Augustus's black skin put in front of him, even in the Catholic Church. Fr. Richardt, one Augustus's professors, had one last card to play. He knew that the Father General of the Franciscans in Rome was a personal friend of Cardinal Simeoni, prefect of the Urban College. Fr. Richardt wrote to him. He explained in detail Augustus perseverance, virtue, progress in his studies, and the impossibility of him attending seminary in the United States. Then he asked the superior of the Franciscans to plead Augustus's case one more time to the cardinal. Augustus was accepted to the Urban College. He left for Rome on February 17, 1880.

Rome opened up a whole new world to Augustus. He roamed the city on his free days, sketching buildings and ruins and recording their history. He learned to play the accordion and enjoyed the international fraternity and cosmopolitan atmosphere of the Urban College and its surroundings. Among his fellow seminarians, he was "Gus from the U.S.," perhaps less advanced in scholarship than many of the others, but above average in virtue.

"Everyone loves me and I don't know why," he wrote to his mentors back in Quincy.

Priests trained at the seminary under the Congregation for the Propagation of the Faith vowed to go wherever that congregation sent them and stay there unless otherwise ordered. Though the United States was still considered a mission land, all indications from his superiors pointed toward Africa as Augustus's future destination. This had been in Augustus's mind, too, for the five years he had thought he would join the Mill Hill Fathers. On the eve of their ordination, Good Friday 1886, Cardinal Giovanni Parocchi met with each seminarian to give him his missionary assignment. At the last minute, the cardinal explained, it had been decided that Augustus should return to the United States, specifically, the Diocese of Alton, Illinois.

"America had been called the most enlightened nation in the world. We shall see if it deserves the honor. If the United States has never before seen a black priest, it must see one now," Cardinal Simeoni had declared.

The cardinal had laid down the challenge, but it would be Augustus who would have to see it through.

The next day, Augustus was ordained a priest in the Basilica of St. John Lateran.

Initially, the reception in America seemed warm. Fr. McGirr had decided Augustus's return warranted celebration. Hundreds of people of both races and all ethnicities lined the streets to cheer the carriage drawn by white horses that took the new priest from the train station to St. Boniface. Augustus then blessed all those who had come to meet him, starting with his mother. He was installed as pastor of St. Joseph's Church in Quincy a few weeks later.

Augustus had actually been instrumental in starting the parish he now had charge of. St. Joseph's was an old Protestant church that the parish of St. Boniface had bought more than a decade before and briefly used as a school. When Augustus was a student at St. Francis Solanus College, it stood empty. He suggested to Fr. Richardt and Sr. Herline that they could use it as a Sunday school for black Catholics. The pastor of St. Boniface granted permission. Augustus rounded up children and convinced parents how important a Catholic education was. Eventually, it grew into a regular day school. While Augustus was in Rome, the school's fortune varied. It closed for a couple of years for lack of personnel, but then reopened as a parish serviced by the priests from St. John's and St. Boniface. Weekly confessions, two Sunday Masses, and vespers were celebrated at St. Joseph's for a couple of years. The school persisted, but when the other parishes lacked priests to help out, services became irregular until Augustus was assigned as its dedicated pastor.

Fr. Gus, as everyone called him, brought new life to the parish. The local newspaper reported that the new priest had "fine educational training," "wholehearted earnestness," and "a rich voice which falls pleasantly on the ear." The pews were full every Sunday for Mass and vespers, and people of both races lined up for Confession. Though the parish was understood as the Negro apostolate, many whites attended too. The choir and the ladies' sodality had members of both races. For Augustus, this was fine. He believed the position of the church was always to welcome, and the additional membership of whites helped support a parish that would otherwise have had a very small and poor congregation. But a year into his ministry, Augustus was discouraged. He reported in his annual update to the Congregation for the Propagation of the Faith that he had only made six converts among African Americans that year. He also noted that he had heard that Archbishop Feehan of Chicago had appealed to Rome to have him sent there. For now, the Congregation replied, keep on doing your good work in Quincy.

By 1887, Augustus's old mentors had all been transferred out of Quincy and a new bishop, John Ryan, appointed to the diocese. St. Boniface also had a new pastor, Fr. Michael Weiss, who was named dean. This new priest was probably the only Catholic in town to harbor a genuine and deep dislike for Fr. Gus. In private, he referred Augustus as "the nigger priest." In public, he made it clear that St. Joseph's was only for black Catholics. He announced from the pulpit that any donations made by whites to St. Joseph's rightfully belonged to St. Boniface. As dean of Quincy, he also informed Augustus that he was only expected to minister to blacks, and he must stop accepting whites into his parish. Augustus said nothing about the issue to his congregation. He did indeed focus his ministry where he knew it was most needed, but he couldn't turn people away who came freely to his church. Augustus was then called to Alton. Bishop Ryan told him "to stop luring whites to his parish or leave." Back in Quincy, Fr. Weiss repeated the bishop's injunction from the pulpit.

Little by little, most of the white parishioners left St. Joseph's. As the parish treasury dwindled, Augustus had to accept invitations to lecture across the country to sustain himself and the church. He traveled to Baltimore at the invitation of Cardinal Gibbons, spoke at the first Black National Catholic Congress in

Washington, D.C, and went to Texas, among other places. When he returned from his lecturing tour, Fr. Weiss's opposition had become an all-out persecution. He wanted nothing less than for Augustus to leave the diocese.

"There is a German priest here who is jealous and contemptuous," Augustus wrote in his second report to the Congregation. "He abuses me in many ways and has told the bishop to send me out of this place. I would gladly leave here just to be away from this priest. I appealed to Bishop Ryan and he also advises me to go elsewhere."

Rome wrote to Bishop Ryan for an explanation.

"Fr. Tolton is a good priest, but he wants to create a kind of society which is not feasible in this place," was the bishop's explanation.

Augustus's superiors told him to accept Archbishops Feehan's invitation and to go to Chicago "at once."

In Chicago, Augustus rented a tiny, cold water flat in one of the black districts of the city and was given charge of all black Catholics in Chicago. The apostolate Fr. Gus inherited consisted of the St. Augustine Society, an association formed some years before by a priest and black Catholics from different parts of the city. As there was no Catholic Church yet in any black neighborhood, they used the basement of St. Mary's at ninth and Wabash to celebrate Sunday Mass. Augustus knew the first thing his parish needed was a church of its own. He had in mind a fine, grand structure, but for the moment, he rented a storefront in his neighborhood. This became St. Monica's. His mother and sister soon joined him from Quincy.

Over the next six years, Fr. Gus wore himself out. He celebrated Mass and heard confessions, visited his parishioners and neighbors, taught catechism, gave homilies, fought alcoholism, succored poverty, continued to give lectures, fundraised, and built a new church. He spent little time with his fellow priests. Chicago did not have the colorblind fraternity of the Urban College.

His parishioners started to notice he sometimes broke out in an unexplainable sweat or had to sit down to give the homily. During the historic heat wave of 1897, he left for his annual retreat. When he returned to Chicago a week later, it was 104 degrees. He started walking home one day from the train station and collapsed. Some bystanders took him to the hospital. His fever mounted, burning the life out of his body. He died on July 9, 1897, with his mother and sister by his side. He was forty-three years old. An overflow crowd attended his funeral at St. Monica's, and even the police department sent representatives. As requested, he was buried in Quincy.

He was declared venerable in 2019.

~

Prayer for the Intercession of Venerable Augustus Tolton

O God, we give you thanks for Your servant and priest, Fr. Augustus Tolton, who labored among us in times of contradiction, times that were both beautiful and paradoxical. His ministry helped lay the foundation for a truly Catholic gathering in faith in our time. We stand in the shadow of his ministry. May his life continue to inspire us and imbue us with that confidence and hope that will forge a new evangelization for the Church we love.

Father in Heaven, Fr. Tolton's suffering service sheds light upon our sorrows; we see them through the prism of Your Son's passion and death. If it be Your Will, O God, glorify Your servant, Fr. Tolton, by granting the favor I now request through his intercession (mention your request) so that all may know the goodness of this priest whose memory looms large in the Church he loved.

Complete what You have begun in us that we might work for the fulfillment of Your kingdom. Not to us the glory, but glory to You O God, through Jesus Christ, Your Son and our Lord; Father, Son, and Holy Spirit, You are our God, living and reigning forever and ever. Amen.

⌒

Please report any miracles or favors to:

Office of the Cardinal
Archdiocese of Chicago
835 North Rush Street
Chicago, Illinois 60611
(312) 534-8376
tolton.archchicago.org

Venerable Theresa Dudzik
Humble Foundress of the Franciscans of Chicago

Born: August 30, 1860 (Plocicz, Poland)
Died: September 20, 1918 (Chicago, Illinois)
Venerated: March 26, 1994 (Pope John Paul II)

"Who is this?" Agnese asked without getting up from her chair in the parlor.

From the window of their apartment, she had seen her daughter leading an elderly woman down the street and into their building. Josephine was now in the hallway, taking her guest as quietly as she could into the kitchen to serve her tea and a piece of the cake without bothering her mother.

"Mrs. Kowalski, mother," Josephine replied without stopping. "Fr. Barzynski said she needs a place to stay."

Josephine hated confrontation, even though she knew she would hear her mother's reproaches later, in private. For now, Agnese sighed and concentrated on darning the sock in her hand.

★ Chicago

They Might Be Saints

Agnese was as devout as the Polish usually are, but she did not approve of her daughter sheltering strangers in their house. There was little she had been able to do to stop it, though, since her husband had died four years ago. Josephine, after all, supported her. Josephine had also been up all night sewing habits for the School Sisters of Notre Dame too. That work, however, would not be compensated, at least not with money.

But Josephine had always been that way. Even as a child, she loved going to church and couldn't stand to hear about someone suffering without responding. She babysat children so harried mothers could go to Mass, shared her lunch at school, and took the spare loaf of bread to the sick neighbor. When she had started to earn her own income as a seamstress, she would buy medicines for the sick. Nothing had changed since the Dudziks had immigrated to the United States in 1881.

Twelve years later, Chicago still teemed with the same hope and poverty as when they arrived. Some people saw their dreams of American prosperity realized, while others found just more work that left them tired, poor, and dirty. A talented seamstress, Josephine was among the lucky ones. Instead of selling her labor dirt cheap in a dangerous factory, she had opened her own dress shop and now had an established, wealthy clientele. While her siblings left for convents or to start their own families, she provided for herself and her parents in comfortable independence.

It weighed on her, though. She couldn't ignore the suffering around her and expect Jesus to welcome her into Heaven. Her disposition to help the poor had turned her into Fr. Vincent Barzynski's unofficial assistant in the parish's charity work. Josephine was well known in the parish overall. St. Stanislaus Kostka was her second home. The largest parish in the country, it was more like a Catholic mansion, or even a small village. Some forty-five organizations operated within it, from sodalities and confraternities to an orphanage, newspaper, four libraries, the biggest auditorium in the city, and a school. Josephine was a member of the choir, superior of both the Young Ladies Rosary Sodality Group II and the Archconfraternity of the Immaculate Heart of Mary. Plus, she was novice mistress for the women's group of the Third Order Secular Franciscans. Still, she wanted to do more to help the poor. Her home was already full, and Josephine's mother complained.

As she had sat sewing the night before, humming to herself, she also imagined a house. In it lived the elderly abandoned by their children who had gone west, childless widows, people crippled by polio, and children born with handicaps. Josephine imagined herself making their beds and gathering them together for prayers. How to accomplish this dream had come to her at prayer the week before. Why not invite her fellow Tertiary Franciscans to purchase a large house together where they could care for these poor people and pray? She also knew several pious women in the parish, some who had even spent several years in religious life, who could teach them about prayer and union with God. She had taken this idea to her good friend and fellow Franciscan, Rose Wisinski, and Rose was enthusiastic, even though she knew she would not be able to join initially because she was already caring for her elderly parents and mute sister.

Josephine presented her idea to the eight tertiaries at their meeting that first Sunday in October. Everyone thought it was excellent, and some, like Josephine, wanted to start right away. Rose, less naïve, proposed that they each pray about it for a year to discern God's will before launching into it. Josephine took this as the will of God and let that thought calm her impatience.

The year passed, and in October of 1894, the monthly meeting fell on the feast of Our Lady of the Rosary. After the usual business, Josephine reminded the women of the plans they had been praying about all year. Some had forgotten completely, but others had kept the idea in mind and were still keen. Josephine asked anyone who was interested and able to submit their names. In the end, all of the tertiaries except Rose offered to join in the project. Now Josephine had to approach Fr. Barzynski, but she was very shy, and it took her a while to work up the courage to speak directly to the priest about her grand idea. She finally seized the opportunity on November 2.

"We're not allowed oppose a good cause," Fr. Barzynski said.

He had only one requirement to give his full approval — the women had to adopt religious life, including vows and a habit. He believed it was the only way they could give the work a firm foundation and lasting future. Josephine had a holy fear of the commitment of religious life, but she reasoned that God would help her. With the priest's guidance, the women started to bring their plans to fruition. Instead of renting or buying a house in Chicago, Fr. Barzynski directed them to build a new house in Avondale, then outside of Chicago. For the time being, they should move into one of their homes for a six-month trial period. As Josephine's home was the largest, they decided it would be hers.

For all of his encouragement, Fr. Barzynski had no illusions about the undertaking Josephine had on her hands. He was a religious, a priest of the Congregation of the Resurrection. He interviewed each of the young woman himself to make sure that they were fully aware of what they were getting themselves into and that they had the right intention. He gave special attention to their leader, Josephine. Did she realize what difficulties she would face in forming these women into a religious community, in serving the poor and gaining the support they would need from the community? Now, when enthusiasm was high, everything seemed easy, but she was subjecting herself to every potential criticism and trial, and she could not abandon the project she had started. That would be worse than never having begun at all.

"You must promise me that you will care for this community not only in its times of prosperity but also when difficulties beset it from all sides."

"I promise," Josephine said.

She did not see what Fr. Barzynski knew was just over the horizon, but she would remember her promise.

On December 8, the Resurrectionist blessed the assembled group and declared it their formal foundation day. One by one, they moved into Josephine's home over the month of December. They elected Josephine their superior and assumed the religious names they had first received when they had first become Franciscan tertiaries, though they still wore lay clothes. Josephine became known as Sr. Theresa. They celebrated that Christmas in a spirit of joy and ease and freedom that Josephine thought would never end.

But if Sr. Theresa had found her mother's complaints sometimes difficult to bear, she now had the sensitivities, needs, and desires of nine women to deal with. They had agreed to put all of their savings in a common fund for the future home for the poor, as well as what possessions they brought and their regular earnings from their work. Sr. Theresa and Sr. Angelina continued their work as seamstresses, plus sewing vestments and altar linens for the church and managing the regular housework. Srs. Francis, Hyacinth, Joachim, and Felixa took on the washing and cleaning for the church and rectory, for which they were paid monthly.

They also followed a daily, communal routine, waking at four thirty in the morning for Morning Prayer and Mass.

Everyone launched wholeheartedly into communal life, except for Sr. Joachim, who refused to open her trunk and share its contents. The discontent among the others at her lack of community spirit quickly grew. Sr. Theresa knew the situation couldn't go on, but she didn't have the courage to take up the issue directly with Sr. Joachim. Instead, she told Sr. Joachim through another sister that she either had to turn her trunk over to the community or leave. Sr. Joachim decided to leave, but not without telling Fr. Barzynski how offended she was that Sr. Theresa didn't deliver the ultimatum to her face to face. The priest called Sr. Theresa to the rectory.

"If you can't tell anyone anything it would be better to disband the community immediately," he said.

Sr. Theresa knew the priest was right. She had to overcome her timidity and her present humiliation.

"I'm sorry, please forgive me," she said clearly and loudly.

The priest's countenance lightened.

Sr. Theresa went home happy, but the honeymoon was over for the forming community. Sr. Hyacinth had become convinced that Srs. Theresa and Angelina were relaxing at home while the other three broke their backs doing laundry and cleaning at the rectory. She said nothing to Sr. Theresa, though, but instead complained to her fellow laundresses. The discord so infected Sr. Francis that it oozed out one morning in an angry vent to Agnese. Sr. Theresa could hear the yelling in the kitchen and went in to find her mother on the verge of tears. Sr. Theresa reassigned herself to laundry duty to give a good example and keep peace. She gave Sr. Hyacinth the sewing and household chores that she had been doing. The doctor had prohibited Sr. Theresa from such physically demanding labor, and she felt sick during the first few days, but she knew as she felt herself adjusting to the work that God was helping her. But still, discontent reigned. Sr. Hyacinth wasn't happy with her new job either, and Sr. Francis was thinking of leaving. Both, along with Sr. Felixa, eventually returned to their own homes. New women joined, but not all of them proved equipped for the community.

Trials came from outside too. Fr. Simon, the priest-treasurer at the parish, paid the sisters for the laundry work, but while both he and Fr. Barzynski were on a leave of absence for health reasons, his substitute told Sr. Theresa that unless they would agree to work for only twenty-five dollars a month, he would replace them. In fact, he had already convinced some other women to take on the job, even though they had initially refused because of the low wages. Sr. Theresa reminded the priest that they had already been paid two months in advance and managed to hang on to the work until the other priests returned. When she got home, Sr. Theresa cried alone in her room, not only at the difficult financial situation this placed them in but also at the slight done to them and their good cause by the priest. But then she sighed, placed everything in God's hands, and told herself that better times would come.

Life goes on even in the midst of trials, she reflected years later, and she was still pressing forward. She had already purchased several lots in Avondale and reminded Fr. Barzynski that they would need a building soon too. They had three people in their care now and a long waiting list of others in need. The priest directed Sr. Theresa to organize a building committee of laymen to manage the business aspects of the project. He also told her that she would need to start begging to raise more money. Sr. Theresa had never anticipated begging. She had always supported herself and her charitable causes by the work of her own hands.

Plus, she was shy. Fr. Barzynski knew it would subject her and the other sisters to ridicule, but he also knew it was necessary.

"Accept the money as a donation for the home, and accept all the rudeness for yourself," he told her.

This inspired Sr. Theresa. On the steps of the city's churches, she and Sr. Agnese received not only hundreds of dollars but also taunts.

In 1897, work on the new building was underway. In the meantime, the women had moved into a larger apartment where they could better care for more elderly and disabled persons. There were years of hard work, between the laundry, the sewing, the planning, and the caretaking. But Sr. Theresa never felt completely spent. She looked forward every day to the evening prayers with the residents, who had at first been indifferent to prayer. Soon, she hoped they would have a proper chapel to pray in. One evening, Sr. Theresa went to inspect the progress. The frame of their future convent and shelter was already erected. She climbed a ladder, looked out over the city, and thought that in a few months God would be praised in this new building. She smiled and cried.

In the spring of 1898, Sr. Theresa and the community moved into St. Joseph's Home for the Aged and Invalids. Rose Wisinski, who had accompanied Sr. Theresa in spirit and in planning the building, finally joined them as Sr. Anna, making the aspiring religious seven. Sr. Theresa's years of patience and perseverance were bringing results, but this new stage brought new trials too. Removed from the city, they had less opportunity for the work that had been supporting them and had very few services nearby for securing their basic needs. They were also far from any church, and since they were not yet officially religious, not having made their novitiate and taken public vows, they did not have a chaplain, regular Mass, nor the Blessed Sacrament reserved. Their situation was more precarious than ever, even as their number of charges increased. Sr. Theresa placed her trust in God. Their material needs she entrusted to St. Joseph, and she had already known that God would supply for her soul even here, far from any church. And so, donations came when least expected, and they moved closer to taking the Franciscan habit.

But in October, the burden of leading the community was lifted from Sr. Theresa. Fr. Barzynski appointed Sr. Anna as superior. That fall, the sisters also received the rule Fr. Barzynski had written for them. On December 8, they would start their postulancy in preparation for receiving the habit as novices. Sr. Theresa took the rule seriously, especially the requirement of silence in the convent, which she considered imperative for spiritual growth. But in the excitement and the novelty of their new home and work, her confreres found it harder to be as recollected as the rule imagined. Sr. Theresa admonished and encouraged her sisters to follow the rule to the letter. In response to the reprimand of her good example, she became the butt of jeers, backbiting, and even gossip by some of the sisters.

Sr. Theresa had not thought religious life would be this way. The idea suddenly came to her to leave. Hadn't she been happier when it was just she living with her mother? She could support them more easily and tranquilly anywhere else. She had done all for the glory of God and wouldn't ask that any of the money she had contributed toward the foundation of the home be returned to her, she told herself. But just when she had found peace in the decision to quietly leave, she remembered that this was what Br. Barzynski had warned her would happen — she would be tempted to forsake the community when things became difficult. And she remembered, too, her promise, and the agony renewed in a cycle that lasted several weeks. She only found peace when she decided to place everything in the hands of God and pray for Him to change the situation. She began to pray for the community more intensely and rely solely on God.

In the years that followed, the Franciscan Sisters of Bl. Kunigunda (later renamed the Franciscan Sisters of Chicago) stabilized and grew, and Mother Mary Theresa's virtues and charismatic inspiration that founded the community would receive their due recognition. In 1900, she was made novice mistress and reelected superior in 1909. Her sisters remembered that she was always first in two things — arriving at the chapel for prayer and taking on the hardest work. She was diagnosed with cancer in 1915, and through her illness kept busy and followed the community schedule. Fr. Andrew Spek, who had become the community's spiritual director after the death of Fr. Barzynski, ordered Sr. Theresa to write a memoir of the founding and first years of the community.

"Those criticisms of my conduct were no small advantage for my pride. I would want to bear more as long as God would not be offended, and I would consider it even greater happiness to be able to suffer for the greater glory of God and the good of the community," she wrote. She had learned to humble herself and trust completely in God.

She died of cancer at age fifty-eight on September 20, 1918. She was declared venerable in 1994.

⌒

NOVENA PRAYER FOR THE INTERCESSION OF
VENERABLE MOTHER MARY THERESA DUDZIK

*Ven. Mother Mary Theresa, during your lifetime you
practiced great charity and later wrote: "I felt the misery*

and suffering of others and was constantly occupied with the thought of how I could be of service to the needy and the poor." I, who venerate you, come to you for help. Ven. Mother Mary Theresa, beg for me at the throne of God, for this, my special intention through Christ our Lord. Amen.

Please report any miracles or favors to:

Franciscan Sisters of Chicago
11400 Theresa Drive
Lemont, IL 60439
(630) 243-3600
mothertheresadudzik.com

Venerable Nelson Baker
Padre of the Poor

Born: February 16, 1842 (Buffalo, New York)
Died: July 29, 1936 (Lackawanna, New York)
Venerated: January 14, 2011 (Pope Benedict XVI)

Nelson pulled his wagon up alongside the two boys coming toward him down the road. The teenagers looked uncomfortable with their heavy sacks, probably full of sugar and salt.

"Where you boys going?" he asked.

"Limestone Hill, St. Joseph's," the taller one with blond hair said.

"Well, me too. Hop in," Nelson replied.

The two heaved their sacks onto the wagon and then made themselves comfortable on the bags of wheat and rye. Nelson slapped the reins, and the horses turned the wagon around to head for the orphanage.

It was 1865, and the boom brought to Buffalo, New York, by the Erie Canal also came with its vices and tragedies, such as abandoned children. In response, the Diocese of Buffalo had built several orphanages. Nelson Baker, then age twenty-five and best known as one of the partners of the feed and grain store Meyer and Baker, had been helping out St. Joseph's Orphanage for years. He donated from the comfortable profits from his business and gave what time he had, too, when the superintendent, Fr. Hines, needed help. From his Lutheran father, Nelson had learned to run a business, and from his Catholic mother, he had learned prayer, charity, and justice. Though baptized in the Lutheran church, he had asked to become Catholic when he was ten.

"Thank you, mister," the boys said and jumped out when they reached the front of the orphanage's two-story building.

Fr. Hines had seen the wagon pull up.

"Nelson," he called out. "What brings you here today? Why don't you come in for a drink?"

"Well, thank you, Fr. Hines," he said and climbed down.

The two settled into the parlor and a conversation that started with small talk turned to other topics.

"Fr. Hines, how hard is it to learn Latin?" Nelson asked.

"It's tedious, but with study and practice it comes. If I could learn it, anyone can. Why do you ask?"

Nelson confessed a recurring thought he'd had for the last several years—he should become a priest. Every time he considered applying to the seminary, though, he remembered that he didn't have the kind of education required to enter the seminary. "*Et cum spiritu tuo*" was about all the Latin he knew, he joked. At the end of their conversation, Fr. Hines sent him home with a Latin grammar book and the promise to write him a recommendation for the seminary. Nelson had no idea learning Latin would later lead him back to Limestone Hill.

For the next year, Nelson spent his evenings, nights, and early mornings studying Latin. By June, he was exhausted and ill. He asked his partner at the store if he could manage the business alone for a couple of weeks. Nelson needed time to rest and reassess if the priesthood was indeed his calling. He took a cruise around the Great Lakes, using the time away from work and home to pray. When he got back to Buffalo, he applied to the seminary. Nelson's mother was delighted — she had been praying for years that he would become a priest. Nelson's younger brother Ransom took over as the Baker in "Meyer and Baker," and Nelson entered the seminary.

His months of lonely Latin studies had paid off, and he did well in his classes. He was about ten years older than most of the other seminarians, but he didn't let the age gap become an obstacle to comradery with them, and he also stood out as a leader. About halfway through his studies, he read that the diocese was organizing a pilgrimage to the shrines of Europe. He asked his superiors for permission to go as the seminary representative, paying for the trip himself. Permission was granted.

The European tour covered France and Italy and their most famous shrines, from the tomb of St. Peter in Rome to the humble grotto of Lourdes. One of the first stops was Paris, with the great Notre Dame cathedral and the famous Rue du Bac and the glittering Sainte-Chapelle. For Nelson though, the less spectacular shrine of Our Lady of Victory, a church built in the seventeenth century to thank the Queen of Heaven for the victories of the French king, was his favorite. Not even Rome itself trumped this shrine for the seminarian. He had placed himself under the patronage of Our Lady of Victory and would be faithful to her his whole life.

Nelson was ordained on March 19, 1876, and his first assignment was Limestone Hill. Fr. Hines was still director of the charity home for boys, but the bishop had placed Fr. Baker there to help, hoping his business experience would re-float the charity drowning in debt. But Fr. Baker couldn't see a way out of financial trouble and asked for a transfer not long after beginning his assignment. It was granted, but the bishop was still convinced that Fr. Baker was the man for Limestone Hill. A year later, he transferred the young priest back as superintendent after reassigning Fr. Hines.

The institution consisted of two sections, the orphanage for boys who had been abandoned or lost their parents, and St. John's Protectory for boys who had gotten into trouble with the law. As the new superintendent, the first thing Fr. Baker did was take the bars off the windows of the protectory.

"There are no bad boys," he said to those who questioned his wisdom.

He wanted both the orphanage and the protectory to be more homelike.

Next, Fr. Baker had to address the creditors breathing down his neck. By now the home owed over sixty thousand dollars (an exorbitant amount of money for that time) to various entities. Fr. Baker looked at the books and made all the adjustments he could. He squeezed out something of the money owed, but certainly not all of it. He was perfectly honest with the creditors. This was the small amount of money he could offer them now, would they accept and allow him more time to continue to pay them back? They all responded with a blunt no. Fr. Baker then hitched the carriage and rode into Buffalo. At the bank where he had his personal account, he took out everything, every last penny in his name. The creditors would have to be satisfied with that.

That evening, he knelt down in front of the statue of Our Lady of Victory he had brought back from Paris and prayed. A plan started to form that would not only save the orphanage and protectory but also fundamentally change fundraising. For the next several months, he collected the addresses of women throughout the country known for their charity. To each of them, he sent a letter explaining the work of St. Joseph's Orphanage and St. John's Protectory and inviting the recipient to become a member of the Association of Our Lady of Victory for an annual membership due of twenty-five cents. Within a few years, he had paid off the debt and raised enough money to build a badly needed extension for the growing number of boys.

Fr. Baker then got another inspiration. In the 1890s, natural gas was found in Buffalo. While paying the large gas bill one evening, he wondered if he might not be sitting on his own store of energy. He investigated the possibilities and took the idea to his patroness. Reassured that he may never need to pay another gas bill again, he asked his bishop for permission to take out a loan to drill for natural gas on the property. Anyone else would have been directly refused, but the bishop knew that Fr. Baker had a way of pulling money seemingly out of thin air. A few weeks later, a crew arrived to start drilling.

"Where do you want us to dig, Fr. Baker?" the foreman asked.

"Follow us," he said.

Coming into the field was a train of altar boys and candles. The foreman and his crew fell in behind the Rosary procession that Fr. Baker led through an open field. After several decades of the Rosary, Fr. Baker stopped the procession and put a small statue of Our Lady of Victory in the weeds and grass.

"Drill here," he told the foreman, "But try not to disturb the statue."

Days into drilling, no gas had been found, and the money was running out. Word spread around Limestone Hill of "Fr. Baker's folly." But Fr. Baker told the crew to keep drilling, and he prayed. At the extraordinarily deep point of 1,137 feet, natural gas finally floated out of the bedrock. They named it Victory Well, and it provided the gas needs for all of the orphanage and protectory, plus fifty houses nearby. The well still produces today.

Fr. Baker was now on his way to building his City of Charity. The number of boys in the protectory had tripled, and the orphanage had doubled in the fifteen years since Fr. Baker had taken over as superintendent. He had also added a trade school, farm, and working boys' home. Legally, the boys in the orphanage and protectory could only stay until they were seventeen, leaving them with little assistance in making the transition to self-supporting adults. The trade school and working boys' home filled this gap so the young men could learn professional skills and have a safe home until they had made their way in the world.

The Erie Canal was also being dredged in the first years of the twentieth century. It shocked the community when among the mud were found the bones and bodies of infants and children. Most likely, they had been thrown into the water by unwed mothers abandoned by family and society. Fr. Baker decided to build a home for these women and their babies. The Infant Home, and later its maternity hospital, welcomed pregnant women and mothers along with their infants. For those too afraid to ask for help, there was a crib inside the unlocked door to safely leave a child in the anonymity of the night. The new ministry caused quite a stir in Buffalo. Critics believed that these women needed to be punished for their sin, even if it meant hard poverty for them and their children. Fr. Baker saw things differently.

By now everyone around Buffalo knew who you were talking about when you said, "Fr. Baker." The orphanage and its attached charities were known simply as "Fr. Baker's." Besides the boys' and maternity homes, the City of Charity provided meals, clothing, and money to countless numbers of people down on their luck. Fr. Baker gave generously, indiscriminately, and with empathy. The priest and superintendent regularly accompanied the Sisters of St. Joseph, who helped run the institutions, on their begging outings around Buffalo. Then he would go down the bread line, talking to the men and handing out quarters. With each quarter, he hoped he gave them a little self-respect. Anyone who needed help could find it at Fr. Baker's, no questions asked. As with the maternity home, he knew not everyone agreed with his way of doing charity.

"I've often been criticized for taking care of these poor people," he told a friend one day:

> But let's put ourselves in their position. Some of them may have been careless. Some may even have been lazy and didn't want to work and some maybe couldn't find work. They are hungry and cold. What would we do if we were hungry and cold and had no means to take care of ourselves? We would probably go to the corner store and steal a loaf of bread or a bottle of milk and get into trouble. We do this for these men to keep them from getting into trouble.... God is blessing our work. Times are hard but we manage. When I die the Lord will not ask me if all of them were worthy, but he might ask me if I gave.

It was now 1921, and Fr. Baker was seventy-nine years old. Despite decades of indefatigable labor, he still had one dream he wanted to accomplish. Now was the time, he decided, to tear down the old St. Patrick's parish church and erect a fitting tribute to the intercessor who had made the City of Charity possible.

He sent a letter to the Association of Our Lady of Victory, by now numbering thousands of members, asking for donations to build a church in honor of their patroness. It wouldn't be just another church but rather a grand one. As architect he chose Emile Uhlrich, the famous French church builder. With the architect, Fr. Baker watched over every detail of the building from materials to design. When it was consecrated in 1926, its dome was the second largest in the United States, just behind that of the nation's capital building. Two years later, Pope Pius XI raised it to a minor basilica.

On the heels of completing the church followed the Great Depression. Though now in his eighties, Fr. Baker was far from slowing down. He organized the distribution of hundreds of thousands of meals, as well as providing clothing and medical care, each year of that difficult time.

People also spoke of miracles worked through him, whether through his prayers or the novenas to Our Lady of Victory prayed with the association. According to one account, there was a nurse from the maternity home who had died. She had already been pronounced dead, but after Fr. Baker prayed the Rosary by her bedside, she revived.

In 1936, Fr. Baker finally slowed down, and he died on July 29. Half a million people came out for his funeral, and more claims of miracles followed quickly after his death.

Fr. Baker's cause for sainthood was opened in 1987, and in 1999, his body was transferred to the Basilica of Our Lady of Victory. When it was disinterred, it was found that his blood had been put in a vial and placed in its own casket, as is typically done for European royalty. Fr. Baker's blood was not dried as would be expected but still liquid.

He was declared venerable in 2011.

☞

Prayer for the Beatification of
Venerable Nelson Baker

*Lord, you gave us Your Servant Nelson Baker as an
example of service to the poor, homeless, and the young.
By "Fr. Baker's" ardent concern for those in need, inflame
our hearts and lives with compassion for the poor, justice for
the oppressed, hope for the troubled, and courage to those
in doubt. We pray through the intercession of Our Lady of
Victory, if it be Your will, that Your Servant, Nelson Baker,
may one day be canonized. Amen.*

Glory Be (three times)
Our Lady of Victory, pray for us.

☞

Please report any miracles or favors to:

OLV Charities
780 Ridge Road
Lackawanna, NY 14218
(716) 828-9648
fatherbaker.org

Venerable Maria Kaupas

U.S. Immigrant Housekeeper Turned Foundress

Born: January 6, 1880 (Ramygala, Lithuania)
Died: April 17, 1940 (Chicago, Illinois)
Venerated: July 1, 2010 (Pope Benedict XVI)

"Always more, always better, always with love."

The oft-repeated motto and way of life of Ven. Mother Maria Kaupas, the future foundress of the Sisters of St. Casimir, seems to have been instilled in her from her earliest days of childhood. She was born Casimira Kaupas into a farming family of eleven children in Ramygala, Lithuania in 1880. Their profoundly religious family was led by her father singing the Psalms throughout the day and her mother consistently demonstrating care and compassion within the family and community.

★ Chicago

Casimira was a devout child who was attentive to the role of God in her life. She was a happy young woman, spending days on the farm tending the animals and enjoying books, as she was an avid reader. But she left her simple life behind when she came to the United States in 1897 at the request of her older brother, Rev. Anthony Kaupas, to serve as his housekeeper while he was pastor of St. Joseph Lithuanian parish in Scranton, Pennsylvania. When she arrived, her brother was astonished to see in front of him not the little farm girl he once knew but, instead, a fashionable young lady with stylish clothes and a straw hat.

Casimira enjoyed her first days in the United States but began to witness the difficulties and hardships of the Lithuanian immigrants in the United States. Most of the fathers were miners, and a large number of them were killed in the hazards of the work. As a result, many young women became widows, and children were without parents. Casimira, with all her heart, wished she could do something for them. How could they be helped to keep their faith? And maintain their language and their culture?

It was during this four-year stay in Scranton that Casimira witnessed women in habits for the first time and became attracted to an apostolic religious life. She was inspired by the sisters that she saw in Scranton and asked her brother who they were, as she had never seen women members of a religious community in her life. He told her that they are "women who live for God alone." After some discernment and reflection, she realized that if she were to enter religious life, she would be able to find a way to help these people for whom her heart was grieving. When she told her brother of her intent to enter a community in the United States, he informed her that the American Lithuanian clergy sought to establish a Lithuanian congregation of women religious for the purpose of educating the youth in a Catholic setting and preserving the Lithuanian language and customs. Casimira was then asked to lead this new venture that would sustain and nourish the faith of the early Lithuanian immigrants in the United States.

Even when she had returned to Lithuania and as many pieces seemed to be quickly falling into place, she momentarily began to question the meaning of her participation in all of it. While on the night train leaving Lithuania, she tearfully began journaling: What am I doing? Why am I leaving my homeland? Moving beyond these emotions, she reminded herself that she was doing this all for God and that for Him nothing is ever enough. She later wrote, "I will not be stingy with God, but having offered Him all, I will persevere in doing His will."

Casimira spent three years in Ingenbohl, Switzerland, where the Sisters of Mercy of the Holy Cross taught and prepared her for the work to which she felt called. In 1905, with the help of her brother, she found a priest, Rev. Dr. Anthony Stanuikynas, who would help shape the congregation as an educational leader and spiritual guide. In the meantime, she had found two other women from Lithuania who were willing to join her. Approved in April 1907 by Pope Pius X, the Congregation of the Sisters of St. Casimir was established on August 29, named for the patron saint of Lithuania at the insistence of Bishop John W. Shanahan of Harrisburg, Pennsylvania, despite Casimira's wish that the congregation be named after the Mother of God. She still found a way to honor the Virgin Mary under the title of the Immaculate Conception: Casimira took the name Sr. Maria, and her two companions became Srs. M. Immaculata and Concepta as they started their lives anew in the congregation.

The dream had become a reality—but now the hard and unknown work of getting a religious community off the ground and flying was yet to come. Mother Maria fashioned the spiritual identity of the congregation. She taught the Sisters the mission, entrusted to them by the Church, that works of faith and love must flow from a life of union with God rooted in faith, built on love, and imbued with a spirit of hope. Mother Maria also had a great sense of humor, and her spirited laugh enlivened the growing congregation.

She inspired the community and offered them a personal motto: "Fortified with a good intention, wherever you are and whatever you do, always keep it in mind: God is here!" She was often seen by the other sisters late at night in deep prayer in the presence of the Eucharist: "What happiness will be ours as we work in union with him ... our dearest Friend! After our daily tasks are completed, what joy we shall experience as we rest at his feet ... and lovingly converse with him!" Mother Maria was always responsive to the Holy Spirit and lovingly accepted the valuable assistance and religious training from the Sisters of the Immaculate Heart of Mary at Marywood in Scranton. Mother Cyril, their General Superior, greatly supported and befriended this new community founded under Mother Maria's care, and a friendship arose between the communities that persists even to this day.

In seeking to ameliorate the plight of the Lithuanian immigrant, Mother Maria decided to start first with the education of children, who would then share their knowledge and faith with their parents. From Scranton, Mother Maria traveled to Mount Carmel, Pennsylvania, where Fr. Stanuikynas was pastor, to prepare for the opening in 1908 of the congregation's first parish convent and school, opening with over seventy pupils. The establishment of Holy Cross school made an imprint not only on the local Catholic community but also on the entire community of mostly poor mining families.

In 1916, the bishops of Lithuania wrote to Mother Maria seeking her assistance. They had heard about the great advancement that she and her sisters had made amongst the Lithuanian-American immigrants and asked that she return to Lithuania and establish her congregation there. In 1920, Mother Maria sailed to Lithuania with four of her sisters and, within weeks, new candidates arrived in the congregation. As the sisters increased in number, they opened schools and other institutions in various cities throughout the country.

Lithuanian pastors throughout the United States too began recognizing the depth and strength of this new congregation of women religious working toward preserving the faith life of the immigrant people. They sent requests begging for sisters to staff their parochial schools: first in Pennsylvania, later in Chicago and in many other parts of the country. Mother Maria herself traveled by train to the East Coast to visit these missions and offer support to the sisters, both for their religious formation and education, as she would be seeking to send them for college degrees in Chicago. When bishops asked various communities to send people to the missions in New Mexico, Mother Maria responded and, despite the fact that there were no Lithuanians there, she sent her Sisters to learn to speak the language and to minister to the people there.

Because of the large concentration of Lithuanian immigrants in Chicago and considering the advantages for the Sisters to be more centrally located, Bishop Shanahan consented to have the Sisters build their motherhouse in Chicago. It was completed on February 28, 1911, and St. Casimir Academy was opened in the building on September 5 of that same year. The first classes were composed of preschool children and grammar and high school pupils. Some were boarders at St. Casimir Academy and continued at the high school within the motherhouse facility until 1952, when the Maria High School was built to accommodate the growing number of girls seeking a Catholic education under the direction of the Sisters of St. Casimir.

More and more Lithuanian men across the country were finding vocations, and these new priests were beginning to build schools with their parishes. There came many opportunities in Pennsylvania and in New England, where there were many Lithuanian immigrants in parishes that correspondingly were beginning to request sisters for the schools. In Newtown, Pennsylvania, northeast of Philadelphia, Mother Maria, in a display of business acumen and foresight, purchased 206 acres of beautiful farmland for the mission of the congregation and turned it into Villa Joseph Marie High School, a school for young women opening in 1932.

For the first twenty years, the Sisters of St. Casimir were focused in the United States on education as their primary apostolate. When the United States experienced the influenza epidemic of 1918 to 1919, it was evident to Mother Maria that there were too few doctors and too few to give care. Responding to growing healthcare needs, Mother Maria prepared her sisters as nurses and administrators to staff Holy Cross Hospital, which was built in 1927 and opened in 1928. The congregation took ownership of Chicago's Loretto Hospital (formerly the Francis Willard Hospital) in 1938. Bishop George Mundelein had seen the great opportunity for the presence of a Catholic hospital in Chicago, so he sent out a request to all of the communities who already ran hospitals to put in their bid to staff it. When Mother Maria chose not to send in a letter, he personally phoned her to submit her bid. Within two weeks, she received a response that she was given the hospital.

In 1932, Mother Maria felt a lump that caused her to go to the hospital, where she had it removed. It was diagnosed as cancer, and the doctors felt that they had taken care of it. She continued to monitor it over the years. Gradually, when arthritis affected her hands and bones elsewhere, she had pain radiating throughout her system. Within a few months of the celebration of the twenty-fifth anniversary of the congregation, it became evident that Mother Maria was suffering from a malignant condition. Her deep prayer life sustained her. She persevered with inspiring serenity for the next eight years and showed great courage as the bone cancer spread—the disease that had started in her breast had metastasized to her bones.

On April 17, 1940, after having prayed that her suffering that very day be united to that of Christ on the Cross, Mother Maria passed on to her eternal reward at the motherhouse, surrounded by her sisters. She had served in the office of General Superior for twenty-seven years, from 1913 to her death. It was commonly accepted amongst the sisters, priests, and laity who knew Mother Maria that she was a very holy person. Within a matter of hours after her death, the newspapers carried articles, with headlines like "Sainthood Sought for Mother Maria" and "Chicago mourns its second Cabrini." Thousands of people came for her wake and burial.

Mother Maria Kaupas was declared venerable in 2010.

⁓

PRAYER FOR THE INTERCESSION OF VENERABLE MARIA KAUPAS

Gracious God, we praise and thank You for Your faithfulness and love. You have blessed us with the example of Your servant, Maria Kaupas, whose deep faith in Your presence, love for the Eucharist, and zeal in fostering the faith life of others continues to inspire us. Through her intercession, we pray that (make your request). Help us to continue life's journey with a heart filled with a profound faith in You and that trust which is born of love. We ask this through Jesus our Lord and the power of the Holy Spirit. Amen.

⌒

Please report any miracles or favors to:

Sisters of St. Casimir
2601 W. Marquette Road
(773) 776-1324
Chicago, IL 60629
SistersofStCasimir.org

Venerable Norbert McAuliffe

The Missionary of Northern Uganda

Born: September 30, 1886 (Manhattan, New York)
Died: July 3, 1959 (Alokolum, Gulu, Uganda)
Venerated: May 19, 2018 (Pope Francis)

Classes and sports were done, the students had gone home, and the hot Ugandan day was cooling off. Br. Geoffrey and Br. Norbert left the secondary school for the convent. Br. Geoffrey always enjoyed the evening walk with the veteran missionary, the founder and humble leader of the work of the Brothers of the Sacred Heart in Uganda. Many considered Br. Norbert a holy man. He was so calm and strong, so prayerful and joyful, so ascetic and kind, so perceptive and peaceful. They arrived at the convent with time before the community's evening prayer, but Br. Norbert went straight to the chapel. With reason, the Ugandans had long ago named him Dano Ma Lego, "The Man Who Always Prays." It was a habit he had had since his novitiate fifty

New York ★

years ago. Perhaps it started even further back, in his childhood with the Dominicans.

Born in 1886, as a nine-year-old then known by John, his baptismal name, Br. Norbert went to live at St. Agnes Home for Children run by the Sparkill Dominicans. His Irish immigrant father and American mother had both died suddenly in the year before. John and his brother were taken in by the Dominicans. Life at the orphanage was a scheduled flow of learning, working, playing, and praying. John was a good student, but his first passion was baseball. He played shortstop, and his quick Irish temper rose up in defense of his team in disputes over plays.

After six years under the care of the Dominicans, he found a new passion and his vocation. Fr. Stanislaus Keating, a Brother of the Sacred Heart, came to talk to his class one afternoon about the work of the community. They had been founded in France a century before to teach and care for poor children and orphans. Now they were missionaries, and in the United States, they were opening new schools and orphanages in the South. John told Fr. Stanislaus that he, too, wanted to be a Brother of the Sacred Heart. A few months later, the sixteen-year-old John was discharged from St. Agnes Home for Children and entered the juniorate of the Brothers of the Sacred Heart in Metuchen, New York.

Along with John, eleven other young men also started down the path of religious life in 1902. They were the first group of novices at the community's new formation house. They helped work the farm that sustained the community and studied in preparation for their lives as teachers. On November 21, 1903, John McAuliffe, now Br. Norbert, took his religious vows. He then launched into teaching, starting with the sixty first and second graders at St. Patrick's school in Indianapolis, Indiana.

Formal education at the beginning of the twentieth century was still very different from what it is today. A century ago, many people successfully carried out professions that today require a college degree without even finishing high school. As a religious, Br. Norbert had a community of experienced teachers to guide him in the teaching profession, and he studied independently, as well. While engaged in the community's apostolate and religious life, Br. Norbert also slowly added the professional training of the time, such as high school and teacher's college, to his expertise. He was then assigned to the school in Washington, Indianapolis, where he spent twelve years, the last six as director. In 1920, the Brothers were offered the opportunity to attend Loyola University in New Orleans. Br. Norbert eagerly accepted. He graduated with a bachelor of science degree that qualified him to teach higher-level English, Latin, chemistry, math, and physics.

Br. Norbert had a natural talent for teaching. He won his students' confidence and threw interesting anecdotes into his lectures to keep their attention. In religion class, he transformed when he spoke about the love of God, and his sincere enthusiasm kept his pupils transfixed. For Br. Norbert, everything related to God. Language helped man communicate with Him. Through geometry, he could find God everywhere. Biology and chemistry showed God's creative power and warned men of the destructive consequences of misusing it.

In 1930, Br. Norbert left for Renteria, Spain, where the general house of the Brothers of Sacred Heart had been established. It was time for him to make the Grand Novitiate, a nine-month long retreat and study period. He had long wanted to be a missionary and had even contemplated leaving the Brothers of the Sacred Heart for an order of missionary priests. Then, from

America, the provincial superior sent out the call for volunteers to start a mission in Uganda. Br. Norbert responded. He was appointed director of the six chosen brothers. They left for Africa in the spring of 1931, stopping in Lourdes along the way. From Marseilles, they then took a ship to Mombasa, Kenya, and then a train across the country to Soroti, Uganda. There, an Italian missionary priest met them with a car and took them the last 225 kilometers to Gulu, Uganda. They arrived in Gulu on the feast of the Assumption, August 15.

The brothers were in Uganda to take over the teaching and management of St. Louis College. The school had been started by Italian missionary priests, but as Uganda was an English colony, the colonial authorities required English-speaking teachers. Only now, after decades of colonial rule, were the British showing more concern for the northern part of Uganda. Gulu was the principal city of the important agricultural area of the north. Fields of cotton, tea, coffee, corn (maize), sorghum, and tobacco surrounded the city, but it was mainly exploited for the manpower the locals could provide by being recruited into the British army. For missionaries, the situation meant isolation and few resources for carrying out modern education. The post office was five kilometers from the school. Farming and hunting wild guinea fowl had to feed the brothers and their students. The locals had some Christian influence already thanks to previous missionaries, but many of the students they would teach were Muslims. With the Great Depression at its height, finances were tight everywhere too. Br. Norbert got to work with determination, prayer, and peace. The brothers started teaching classes the day after they arrived.

Through the quality of their teaching, the brothers quickly won the respect of the Africans. Of the six brothers, Br. Norbert stood out. He prayed constantly, the rosary beads slipping through his hands and his lips moving silently as he waited for the students to finish an exercise or for the food to be served in the refectory. The community had the custom of taking a needed rest hour after the noon meal, but Br. Norbert spent it praying in the chapel. If he couldn't be found elsewhere, he was almost always in the chapel, so absorbed in prayer he seemed like another statue. He was also a subtle ascetic. At meals, he always took the smallest portion necessary to just satisfy his hunger. He never raised his voice or spoke ill of anyone and ended every conversation with a kind word. He observed his religious life so perfectly, you could set a clock by him, they said. If he was mistaken, he asked pardon with sincere humility.

As administrator and superior, he also had to manage the relations with the Italian priests, the diocese, and the colonial authorities. It could be tricky, but he guarded the needs of the school and the brothers, while also acting with genuine charity toward wider mission needs. He also had to deal with health problems in the community. Br. Norbert himself was blessed to be unaffected by malaria, but other brothers suffered from the African illness. Br. Christopher, especially, had regular bouts of malaria, as well as teeth problems. It was a serious problem for the mission of few men and little money. Br. Norbert wrote to his superior in the United States to send missionaries with strong stomachs and good teeth, but Br. Christopher never heard his superior complain, though his ill health often left the other teachers in a lurch. Whatever problems the brothers or the school faced, Br. Norbert never burdened the brothers unnecessarily with these worries. He was so quiet about difficulties that sometimes his fellow missionaries thought that he was ignorant of obvious problems, but his letters to his superiors in the United States show he handled everything that came up in challenging situations with prudence and insight. Finally, in 1939, Br. Norbert heeded the call of his provincial to return to New York for a needed break.

The outbreak of World War II, though, prevented him from returning to Uganda. Instead, he was made director of the Metuchen community where he had been a novice. Between war rationing and the poverty of the farm meant to feed them, the large community could barely take care of itself. But this was also the moment in history when the techniques of mechanized, high-yield modern farming were being developed and taught at universities. Br. Felix, who ran the farm, asked his superior to be able to attend Rutgers University, and Br. Norbert granted it. By the end of the course, the farm had become completely self-sufficient and productive enough to have a surplus. Br. Pascal, the community tailor, also asked Br. Norbert for permission to take sewing lessons from a professional tailor in New York City. Br. Pascal had little information on exactly who the man was or where to find him, but Br. Norbert ceded to the request anyway. It took Br. Pascal a couple of visits to different tailors before he found the one who had offered him lessons, but in one summer he learned to make professional quality habits in a quarter of the time he had previously spent.

"No other director would have given me the permission," he later admitted to Br. Felix.

"Br. Norbert was a saint, and saints usually see things that normal people aren't capable of," he replied.

The brothers who observed him so often in the chapel wondered what he did in the hours of closed-eye prayer. Br. Camille, a teacher, had the job of chauffeuring Br. Norbert on necessary business. In their drives, their conversations wandered through various themes, usually spiritual ones, as these were the most interesting topics to Br. Norbert.

"What do you do during all the time you spend in the chapel?" Br. Camille finally asked.

"I simply sit and let the love of God come to me from the tabernacle," Br. Nobert said.

The six years that Br. Norbert spent as superior at Metuchen went down in legends as some of the best years for the community.

In December 1945, Br. Norbert sailed from New York back to Uganda to take over as director. The last period of his life would be his most fruitful in his missionary work. During his time in the United States, four Africans had expressed interest in becoming brothers. Br. Norbert officially opened a juniorate for them that school year. Each day after the afternoon tea, he met with them to give spiritual and personal advice and helped them with their studies. The novices came from different regions of Uganda, but under the guidance of Br. Norbert, their differences disappeared. The Brothers' missionary work also expanded to Kenya and Sudan, and new missionaries came from the United States and more African novices joined too.

Unexpectedly, Br. Norbert's health started to decline. In 1952, he weighed barely a hundred pounds. He went to Kenya for an exam and was diagnosed with cancer. He had to return to the United States again. But at the hospital in New Jersey, the doctors couldn't find any of the evidence of the disease that x-rays in Kenya had shown. With rest in Metuchen, he recovered. He also stayed long enough to celebrate the fiftieth anniversary of the first novitiate, his novitiate, at Metuchen. He returned to Gulu at the end of 1953, this time relieved of the duties of director. In 1955, the first group of Ugandan novices he had nurtured took their vows as Brothers of the Sacred Heart.

Br. Norbert was now almost seventy, but he had no intention of retiring from mission life. He dedicated his later years to the novices and supervising the school children at recess.

"The Lord has been sweet with me," he told Br. Howard during the last year of his life.

Three days before he died, Br. Norbert caught a bad cold and went to bed. The next day, he went to Confession and received Holy Communion, but the following day, when Br. Francis Mwai checked on him, he was breathing with difficulty. It was the end. The priest came, and Br. Howard started reciting the prayers for the dying. Br. Norbert died peacefully and without a struggle. It was July 3, 1959.

The Bishop of Gulu asked the Brothers to allow him to celebrate a solemn funeral Mass for Br. Norbert. Like others, he considered the Brothers the most influential force in bringing the gospel to northern Uganda.

After the Mass, the funeral procession followed the casket while praying the Rosary, just like Br. Norbert.

He was declared venerable in 2018.

⁀

PRAYER FOR THE INTERCESSION OF
VENERABLE NORBERT MCAULIFFE

Lord Jesus, You blessed Your servant, Ven. Br. Norbert, with an intimate experience of Your presence and abiding love in the Blessed Sacrament. The love that You nurtured in his heart was brought to fullness through his vocation as a Brother of the Sacred Heart. Through him, You bestowed Your tender love on Your beloved people of Uganda in his ministry of education and formation of the young, and by his attentive presence to all. May this "man who prays" be for each of us an example of faith, love, and hope. Through his gifts of prayer and presence point us toward You, the source of all love. Through his intercession grant us what we pray for (make your request). May the Church, inspired by the Holy Spirit, beatify him as an apostle of the love You bear for all in Your Sacred Heart, You Who live and reign with the Father and the Holy Spirit, now and forever. Amen.

⌒

Please report any miracles or favors to:

Fratelli de Sacro Cuore
Piazza del Sacro Cuore, 3
00151 Roma Italia
http://www.coindre.org/
fscsecretariatgeneral@gmail.com

Venerable Antonietta Giugliano
American-Italian Foundress

Born: July 11, 1909 (New York, New York)
Died: June 8, 1960 (Italy)
Venerated: December 21, 2019 (Pope Francis)

Antonietta put the card with the novena to the Virgin Mary back into the copy of *The Imitation of Christ* that always rested on her nightstand. She knew the prayer by heart, from having recited it so many times, but she still liked the card. When she needed, or even just wanted, something—a virtue, help on a test, or an unimportant trifle—she started the novena. She had never had to pray the whole nine days before the favor arrived. This time, she was praying that it wouldn't rain on the closing celebration of the school year, her last one at the boarding school of the Sisters of Charity in Naples. She loved what she had learned from the sisters. Not just math and history and writing, but the secrets of prayer, the way of the saints, and how

New York ★

to draw closer to God. In this last year, *The Imitation of Christ* and *The Story of a Soul* had been particularly inspiring for her.

The sixteen-year-old had been born in New York in 1909. When she was five, her mother had died, and her father, Francesco Giugliani, a successful businessman, decided to return to their home in Afragola in the province of Naples with her and her two sisters. Now Antonietta was almost grown up, with even features, thick dark hair, and large brown eyes: an Italian beauty with position and money, not a likely candidate for the cloister. But any vocational commitments, whether marriage or otherwise, were still several years away. She wouldn't be an adult under Italian law until she was twenty-one. In the meantime, she would finish coming of age in the family home with her father and stepmother and seven siblings.

She started this new phase with a plan. "Never say news, curiosities, things that happened; never say useless words when nature wants to speak. I will always be collected internally; I will say to myself: the word is silver but silence is gold," she wrote half way down the page. Everything she had learned from *The Imitation of Christ* and *The Story of a Soul* went into her own "Regulation of the Christian Life," as she had entitled her personal commitment to the spiritual life. It listed thirty-two points, from the schedule she would follow to the weekly penances she would do to the habits she would cultivate. Waking up at five thirty in the morning to be at the parish church at six thirty for meditation and Mass drew red flags her family and their expectations for her to marry well and continue to build the Giugliani fortune. She found one confidante in her friend and relative Raffaelina Tuccillo. The two girls spent a lot of time together, and with this younger relative, Antonietta shared her desire to become a cloistered nun and hide herself from the world.

The two girls also took a trip to France and visited a mutual cousin who was a missionary sister. This opened Antonietta's mind to a different way of giving herself to God—hiding herself from the world in a far-off mission land where she could also do active charity. The peace of her cousin had impressed her, and she also had caught something of the missionary spirit then being promoted by Pope Pius XI. Now twenty, and having recently lost her father, she sought guidance in her vocational discernment from her parish priest. He suggested that she go for spiritual direction to Fr. Vicenzo Del Prete, who is on the path to sainthood himself as a servant of God with a cause for canonization underway. The Franciscan and organist and Vicar of the Convent of St. Anthony in Afragola was gaining a reputation for holiness. Fr. Sosio, as he was known, immediately saw Antonietta's courage and energy and wondered if God wasn't calling her to a special mission. Over the next months, he tested her desires and intentions.

Then, in May 1930, Fr. Sosio had his own life-changing moment. In Italy in the early twentieth century, the children of the poor received little education, whether religious or secular, and the changing times had left many behind. In the corners of cities and hidden hamlets, the elderly poor died abandoned in squalor. Fr. Sosio got taken deeply into these places one day when a woman caught him on his way back to the convent and begged him to bring Holy Communion to dying women. He accompanied the woman to a hovel in the tiny village of Lazzaretto and stayed with her until she died. He then obtained permission from his superior to spend several months in a hermitage. He had realized just how much work there was be done in Afragola for the poor, especially the elderly. It also seemed that God might be calling Antonietta to collaborate in it.

When he met with her again in September, he proposed an idea.

"I believe," he told her, "that the apostolate and the congregation that God is calling you to is here in your own country. *The good you want to do somewhere else, needs to be done here.*"

"Do with me what the Lord best inspires you," Antonietta said. "I'm just afraid that given my nothingness, I won't succeed in such a difficult undertaking."

"Abandon yourself, with full confidence, into His hands, and let yourself be guided by Him for the realization of this work which He certainly wants," Fr. Sosio said.

The priest believed God was calling her to found a new community of sisters to care for the poor right there in Afragola and Italy. He gave Antonietta Lazzaretto and its elderly and poor as her first mission.

Back at home, the Giugliano family was shocked. From entreaties and arguments, her brother-in-law eventually resorted to beating Antonietta to deter her from her vocation. Desperate, she ran away and found refuge in a convent in a nearby village.

The result was scandal, with everyone in Afragola wondering who she ran away with. When Raffaelina found out what was going on, she invited Antonietta to live with her. Then, the two started looking for a place to open a hospice. Four other young ladies from wealthy families also became interested in the work. Using the promise of her pending inheritance, Antonietta provisionally purchased a building next to the Franciscan convent. The community made its debut on June 13, the feast of St. Anthony of Padua, begging for alms on the steps of the convent church "in the name of the Institute of the Little Servants of Christ the king."

With the support of a group of Third Order Franciscans, Antonietta and other future sisters turned the old building into a hospice for the elderly and a day care center for children. She was never afraid to try something new: an emergency surgery having to be performed in the bishop's residence inspired her to open a clinic as well. In October 1935, Antonietta took her religious vows as "Antonietta of Jesus." The institute was officially constituted under the Third Order of St. Francis.

However, the reaction from much of the town was anger. Friends of the new sisters' parents told them to take their daughters away from the influence of the "crazy" Fr. Sosio and the "mad" Antonietta. The convent itself was even attacked by arsonists. Luckily, the fire didn't cause any injuries or interrupt the apostolate.

Once Antonietta and the other sisters had won over the people of Afragola, the fascists of the Mussolini regime and then the Second War World challenged her dedication. They attempted to confiscate the building and turn it into their headquarters, but Antonietta defended the poor in her care. During World War II, the convent was also converted into an emergency hospital during the English bombing campaign of 1943. Antonietta and her sisters stayed through the bombardment, administering medicine and tending the wounded. The convent wasn't hit.

After the war, Antonietta focused the work of the Sisters on children orphaned or left destitute by the war, and she expanded the apostolate into other parts of Italy. She opened schools and orphanages, day care centers, and vocational training centers, even collaborating with the national maritime institute and the dental technicians' organization. Her crowning project was rebuilding the Marian shrine in Boscoreale, the Shrine of Our Lady Liberator from the Scourges. She felt honored to be entrusted with the shrine and promoting devotion to Blessed Virgin. Devotion to Our Lady Liberator from the Scourges became a hallmark of the spirituality of the institute.

Antonietta cultivated a spirit of joy, friendship, and cooperation among her sisters. In the convent, the sisters took turns with the daily tasks, Antonietta always giving herself the most difficult, least desirable, and most mundane. She had also long been plagued with chronic pain, and the disease it brought would cause her early death at the age of fifty-one. Her strength fading, she wrote her last testament to her sisters:

> I kneel before all my Sisters as I was able to do in the last General Chapter. If my blessings are worth anything before the face of God, I invoke the blessing of God on the Little Maidservants of Christ the King, on all my Daughters, who can never be praised and blessed enough for all the ponderous work they carry out silently every day. They always remain in hiding and in the shadows, which is the light of God that he prefers over the darkness of pomp. Blessed be these my Daughters who have been my vital passion, my joy, my hope! May they be blessed more and more as they strive to live according to God in accordance with the seraphic ideal. I implore these blessings for me and for them, for those that will come over time, from the Most Holy Virgin Liberator from the Scourges to whom my Daughters are devoted and attached. To the Blessed Virgin Mary Liberator herself I entrust my benefactors, superiors, friends and, if there are any, even my enemies.

By early June, she was dying. The chaplain came to say Mass in her room and asked her what she wanted him to offer it for. She said, "Only one thing: The will of God." Father proceeded.

In the middle, Antonietta whispered, "God's will be done," and died. I was June 8, 1960. She left behind 200 sisters and postulants, 450 elderly, and 1,500 orphans.

She was declared venerable in 2019.

⌒

Prayer for the Beatification of Venerable Antonietta Giugliano

Father, source of love and God of every consolation, Who enlightens our difficult path with the wonderful light of Your saints and soothes our sufferings with the compassion of their hearts: we thank You for giving Your Church Mother Antonietta Giugliano, an extraordinary testimony of Your mercy. Glorify now Your faithful Servant and grant us, through her intercession, the grace we implore of You with childlike hearts. Through Christ our Lord. Amen!

⌒

Please report any miracles or favors to:

Vice-postulazione delle Cause delle Piccole Ancelle di Cristo Re
Via Marciotti, 4
80047 — S. Giuseppe Vesuviano (NA)
Italy
Tel. e fax: 081.529.75.65
postulazione@fondatori-pacr.it

Venerable William Gagnon, O.H.
Modern Missionary to War-Torn Vietnam

Born: May 16, 1905 (Dover, New Hampshire)
Died: February 28, 1972 (Saigon, Vietnam)
Venerated: December 14, 2015 (Pope Francis)

He had literally worn his heart out. On February 28, 1972, Br. William Gagnon, O.H., collapsed and died. His fellow Brothers Hospitaller of St. John of God buried him in the garden of their convent and hospital near Saigon, and immediately, people started to visit his grave—the Vietnamese novices he had guided into a stable community, children caught in the crossfire of a post-colonial power struggle, the refugees he had nursed back to health from malnutrition, and the soldiers whose wounds he had healed.

In the community of the Hospitallers, those who had known him retold anecdotes of his courage, constant service, and leadership in turmoil. Br. William's good works outlived him, just as he knew they would.

Dover ★

William Gagnon was born in 1905, the third of twelve children of working-class French Canadians who had immigrated to Dover, New Hampshire. He had a deep faith that showed from early on. On day, when William was thirteen, the family was returning from church in their horse-drawn carriage. They could see smoke in the distance. William stayed with his younger siblings while his parents and older brothers ran to fight the wildfire.

"Don't worry," he told his mother "I'll stay here and pray."

No one was injured, and the fire served to uncover fertile land for agriculture.

In his late teens, William joined his father and his older brothers in working at the cotton mill in town and helping to support the family. But he also had another desire: to be a missionary. He applied to the Marists, but he was rejected when a medical exam discovered he had a kidney condition. A few years later, he read a newspaper column about St. John of God, the sixteenth-century Spaniard who had founded a community of brothers to care for the sick. The order intrigued him, and they had missions all over the world. After a visit to the community in Montreal, he entered as a postulant in 1930.

When his father was injured a few months later, family duty called him home temporarily. There were still too many young mouths to feed in the Gagnon household, so he stepped up to help during his dad's convalescence. His father recovered, William returned to Montreal in 1931 and finished his novitiate. He spent the next twenty years working in the Order's hospitals in Canada, as well as serving as provincial in Montreal. His time in Montreal ended in a forced mid-term resignation without just cause. He submitted quietly and signed without question the prepared resignation letter handed to him. Br. William just asked to be transferred out of the city to avoid rumors. At his new assignment, he confided his humiliation to another brother and that he was working through it by prayer and meditation. Then, he volunteered to go to Vietnam, the fulfillment of a long-held desire to be a missionary. Born into a French-speaking family, he could manage the logistics of starting a new community in the unraveling French colony.

Br. William and his fellow Canadian brothers landed in Vietnam in 1952 in the middle of the Indo-China war. The French were trying to maintain a vestige of power against communist forces bearing down from the north. The brothers established a hospital in the war-torn conditions they would work in for the next two decades. They could hear grenades land on the roof and roll off into the grass, guns firing and bombs exploding, sometimes in the distance, sometimes close to home. Br. William placed a statue of Our Lady of Fátima outside the house in the direction of the fighting as protection. Along with his daily prayers to Mary, it worked. When a bomb blew the roof off the hospital, no one was even injured. The brothers cared for everyone, civilian and soldier, regardless of whom they fought for, but they weren't always repaid with kindness. After one man recovered from a serious illness through the brothers' care, he showed their picture to the guerillas. No one knows how he got the picture, but the man's action posed a serious threat to the brothers, from arrest to death. They knew of other priests who had been less careful and died. At the request of the bishop, they left the mission for a few days until the danger had passed. But Br. William's resolve never wavered.

"All of us, we remain religious missionaries and work only for the poor, regardless of what is happening around us," Br. William wrote to his superiors in Canada.

The conflict in the north was creating a stream of refugees flowing south. The brothers moved south too. The mission in Bien Hoa, near Saigon, would become the Vietnamese province of the Brothers Hospitaller and the center of Br. William's work.

He wore many hats—provincial, nurse, general contractor, novice master, fundraiser, and social worker. Br. William had been made provincial of the mission with good reason. He was an excellent organizer and spiritual leader. He led with practicality, simplicity, and humility. He took on the simplest and least desirable tasks—holding a patient's hands, preparing bodies for burial, buying food in the market, serving soup to the tuberculosis patients. He guided the construction of the new hospital, too, including the logistics of getting materials and labor. He joined in the work of making the bricks from sand and water. He salvaged equipment form the American Army, as well. Embittered soldiers laughed at him and his brothers hauling away old office furniture for the hospital. He smiled back. He had the faith and hope to build knowing a bomb could soon destroy everything.

William's strength and peace came from his prayer. The rosary beads slipped through his fingers under his scapular in spare moments. At night, he knelt before the cross in his cell, contemplating the absurd death of Jesus that had nevertheless ended in the Resurrection. In caring for the sick and suffering, he was united with Christ in reparation for the sins of the world. William had been made provincial of the mission for a reason. He was an excellent organizer and spiritual leader, but he considered himself the least of the Hospitallers, most useful in humble tasks and not caught up in the complexities of politics and war theory. He was there to serve Christ in the sick. His leadership and decisions through twenty years of danger and war were guided by his contemplation of the Sacred Heart of Jesus.

Where else could he find anything to make sense of the suffering of the innocent people who came to the hospital every day? The scenes could be heart-wrenching. Thousands of people trying to escape the horrors of war sought medical care, rest, and food at the hospital. Refugees arrived malnourished and exhausted from long marches, perhaps with injuries that hadn't been cured and usually with children. Sometimes there was little that could be done with the few resources they had. Br. William cleared a table so two other brothers could attempt an emergency procedure on a woman with a young child. While the nurses brought the woman to the table, Br. William picked the child up, reassured her that her mother would be alright, and placed the little one with others outside the room. Then he returned to help. The woman asked for Baptism, and Br. William poured the water. That was all he could do. She was already gasping the death rattle. This time, he could only bring the child her mother's body. He walked out of the hospital and cried, for the woman, for the child, and for peace.

At night, he walked to the chapel under the light of exploding artillery and the background noise of bombs, "the concert," as he called it. Again, he prayed for peace, for the deceased, and for the protection of refugees. He was also a peacemaker among his fellow brothers, a diplomatic intermediary armed with prayer. He wanted peace in his community and in each of his brothers. If he heard backbiting or arguing, he redoubled his prayers to the Sacred Heart of Jesus. He was also attuned to those around him and knew how to show compassion to each one. He noticed one young missionary brother especially down. Br. William suspected he was homesick, especially as his relationship with his father had become distant. Br. William encouraged him to write home and reached out himself to the man's uncle, who was one of the Brothers Hospitaller in Canada. Slowly but surely, and even from afar, father and son reconciled.

The conflict and fighting only moved southward through the sixties. As their work became more dangerous than ever, the brothers also started to believe that he had a gifted intuition. On February 1, 1968, seven thousand refugees descended on the hospital grounds. The Chinese New Year was about to begin, and diverse rumors flew. Some said there would be a temporary ceasefire to celebrate the holiday. Others had heard that a brutal attack was in store. Br. William had no idea what would happen, but he knew that without resources to care for so many people, proper hygiene would be impossible, leading to the spread of disease. Br. William told them all to disperse. The next night, the hospital grounds were bombed in the bombardment of Saigon. Those who had refused to leave were killed. Months later, with the fighting no better and the day exceptionally hot, Br. William exempted the community from gathering in the community room for the usual hour of recreation. Had they all been there, they would have become victims of the bomb that hit the community room. Another night, Br. William's peace of heart saved him: The fighting around them was intense, and bullets were hitting the convent. Br. William had always counseled the community to try to sleep through the night and trust that their time on earth was in God's hands. That night, though, with bullets hitting the convent itself, the brothers couldn't sleep, and they went to wake their provincial.

Br. William rose from bed and stood in the doorway of his room. "What's the matter?" he asked.

Suddenly, one of the other brothers jumped at him and pushed him back. A bullet whizzed by them and exploded in the door frame where Br. William had been standing. Br. William got up and sent everyone back to their cells to sleep.

From the beginning, the Hospitallers had also collaborated closely with the Redemptorist Fathers. The brothers made retreats with the priests and also accompanied them into the jungle.

Leaving the city, they went to two of the many tribes in Vietnam to dispense medicines and the sacraments. Br. William was also deeply impressed by his visit to the leper colony run by the Sisters of Charity of St. Vincent de Paul.

After 1970, Br. William's health started to decline. He gave his last months to the mission by doing the simple tasks he had the strength for in the dispensary and apologizing to the community for being a burden. When he died, he was laid out on a bed of tea leaves and a white sheet, and the people he had served insisted on providing him a teak wood coffin. He was buried near the chapel. Today, ex-votos, the testimonies of those who claim to have received favors through his intercession, decorate his grave. He never looked for recognition, but his life of heroic dedication to the sick and poor won him the title of venerable in 2015.

As he had once said, "All worldly honors are nothing but the smoke and fire of burning straw. All that remains is the little good that we have done, if we have managed to make the most of the grace which our good Lord has given us at every instant in our lives."

Br. William had formed the Vietnamese novices who joined the Canadian brothers into a solid foundation to continue the work of the Hospitallers into the future. The mission survived the fall of South Vietnam to the communist Viet Minh and still continues to this day.

⌒

PRAYER FOR THE INTERCESSION OF
VENERABLE WILLIAM GAGNON

Lord, Jesus, Your mercy inspired the Servant of God
William Gagnon to live hospitality with the ill, the refugees,

and the poor. Grant that we may always minister to all suffering people with charity, as did this son of St. John of God.

Lord, hear the prayer that we address to You (make your request) by the intercession of the Servant of God William Gagnon, in order that we may be affirmed in our faith and that Your glory and the joy of the Church may be proclaimed.

Our Father, Hail Mary, Glory Be

☞

Please report any miracles or favors to:

Hospitaller Order St. John of God — U.S. Province
2468 S St. Andrews Place
Los Angeles, CA 90018
stjog.org
usaprov-office@sbcglobal.net
(323) 734-0233

Venerable Fulton Sheen, Bishop
Bishop of the Media

Born: May 8, 1895 (El Paso, Illinois)
Died: December 9, 1979 (New York, New York)
Venerated: June 28, 2012 (Pope Benedict XVI)

"I feel it is time I pay tribute to my four writers—Matthew, Mark, Luke and John" the charismatic bishop joked from on-stage in front of millions of viewers as he won an unprecedented 1952 Emmy Award as the "Most Outstanding Television Personality" for his wildly popular television program *Life Is Worth Living*. His friendly rival NBC's Milton Berle, perhaps the very first major American television star and popularly known as "Uncle Miltie," saw Sheen as his only competition in the coveted Tuesday night slot. The cleric with the mesmerizing gaze, captivating smile, and polished delivery was a natural for television, drawing as many as thirty million viewers each week in a program that spanned half a decade. Presented

New York ★

by the Du Mont Network, the series was an outgrowth of previous failed attempts at a creating a religious program by rotating in a Protestant minister, a Jewish rabbi, and a Catholic bishop. With Sheen on the screen, the program blossomed into what is perhaps the most widely viewed faith-based programming in the history of television.

Before his high profile in the media, Fulton John Sheen came from humble beginnings. He was born the eldest of four sons to devout Catholics Newton and Delia (Fulton) Sheen on May 8, 1895, on a farm outside of El Paso, Illinois. Sheen was a frail infant, prompting his family to move shortly after his birth to Peoria because of his poor health. As an infant, he contracted tuberculosis. Fulton, as he came to be known, despite his baptismal name of Peter John, was enrolled in St. Mary's Cathedral School. There at the Cathedral of St. Mary of the Immaculate Conception, he served as an altar boy at Mass for Bishop John L. Spalding, one of the founders of the Catholic University of America. Perhaps this experience and the tutelage of the bishop were the initial spark for his vocation. Once while serving at Mass when he was eight years old, Sheen dropped and shattered a wine cruet on the floor. Afterward, Bishop Spalding consoled the boy with two predictions for the future: that he would someday study at Louvain in Belgium and, secondly, he told the boy, "Someday you will be just as I am." Spalding seemed to be prescient — both statements came true.

As the valedictorian of the Spalding Institute in Peoria, Fulton excelled in academics and demonstrated a proclivity for public speaking. For college, Sheen enrolled in St. Viator College in Bourbonnais, Illinois and later attended St. Paul Seminary in Minnesota, being ordained a priest of the Diocese of Peoria at the age of twenty-four on September 20, 1919. Afterward, Sheen went on for a year of further studies at the Catholic University of America, where, five years later, he returned to teach for twenty-three years after earning a doctorate in philosophy in Louvain and a doctorate in sacred theology (S.T.D.) in Rome.

Perhaps it was lecturing in theology and philosophy with classes such as Philosophy of Religion, God and Society, and God and Modern Philosophy at the university to classrooms packed with students and visitors alike that honed his skills as a speaker and evangelist and inspired him to take his gift for oratory to the next level. In 1926, Fr. Sheen got his first taste of broadcasting on the radio when he was invited by a New York station to record a series of Sunday evening Lenten sermons. In the summer four years later, Sheen filled in for two weeks to a huge audience response that led to recordings for the popular NBC Sunday night radio broadcast of *The Catholic Hour*, which ultimately reached an audience of over four million listeners and generated as many as six thousand letters a day. He revealed in a 1937 letter to Catholic University Rector Msgr. Joseph Corrigan the demands of his work:

> During the past year letters demanding personal attention have run between 75 and 100 a day.... This coupled with classes never given with less than six hours preparation for each lecture has left me physically exhausted. However, the good to be done is such that one dare not shrink from its opportunities for apostolate.

The weekly program ran until 1950, with Msgr. Sheen (as he was known after 1934) always with an eye on the Gospels, addressing with Thomistic precision topics like Marian devotion, the dangers of communism, and the great social issues of the time. He also began writing two long-running regular newspaper columns: one for secular syndicated newspapers, "Bishop Sheen Writes," and the "God Loves You" column for the Catholic press. He received countless invitations to travel the country to deliver academic lectures, missions, retreats, guest homilies, and commencement addresses at meetings of various Catholic organizations. His future in television awaited with Msgr. Sheen's first broadcasted appearance coming on the world's first broadcast of a Catholic Mass on Easter Sunday on March 24, 1940.

His national profile then increased tremendously as he was appointed auxiliary bishop of New York in 1951, appeared on the cover of *Time* magazine, and started his television show, *Life Is Worth Living*, with millions of Americans tuning in each week. Sheen's only props on the set of the program were chalk and the famous blackboard erased by the "studio angel." He took on a more ecumenical tone, with the program being commercially sponsored and not operating in the framework of a Catholic setting. He frequently employed stories and humor, to the delight of his rapt audiences. Sheen's vast television audience was comprised of more non-Catholics than Catholics, who listened to him because he earned their respect by speaking the truth forcefully and with clarity.

Walking the streets of New York, Sheen would engage with people on the street from all backgrounds and attitudes toward him: admirers, critics, believers, or fallen-away Catholics. There were more than a few angry confrontations on the street. He was a staunch defender of the Faith and famously and frequently reminded people of the evils of communism. He forcefully preached on the existence of absolute truth: "America, it is said, is suffering from intolerance—it is not. It is suffering from tolerance. Tolerance of right and wrong, truth and error, virtue and evil, Christ and chaos. Our country is not nearly so overrun with the bigoted as it is overrun with the broadminded." Despite his tenacity with matters of Church doctrine, his interactions with people were characterized by kindness, sympathy, and his desire to understand the challenges that people were going through. He attracted many to the Catholic Faith, famously asserting that "there are not one hundred people in the United States who hate the Catholic Church, but there are millions who hate what they wrongly perceive the Catholic Church to be." He was involved with some noteworthy conversions, such as politician and U.S. Ambassador Clare Booth Luce, journalist Heywood Broun, activist and writer Louis Francis Budenz, stage designer Joe Mielziner, Communist organizer Bella Dodd, and Henry Ford II. Like any public figure, he was not without his detractors, and the ecclesiastical rivalry between Sheen and Cardinal Spellman was well documented and resulted in his removal from the Archdiocese of New York.

Sheen worked to maintain a strong personal life of faith, engaging in frequent self-examination in the silence of prayer: "Prayer begins by talking to God, but it ends by listening to Him. In the face of Absolute Truth, silence is the soul's language." He went to Confession weekly and maintained a small private chapel with the Blessed Sacrament where he would spend an hour each day in adoration. He reminded his audiences that "the greatest love story of all time is contained in a tiny white Host." The holy hour, in his frequent written and spoken remarks about eucharistic adoration, was an essential part of his routine in his daily life. He also kept as central in his thoughts and presentations the power of the Cross. To get to Easter Sunday, there must be a Good Friday, he would remind his congregations in New York City at Lenten services such as the three-hour-long Good Friday services at St. Patrick's Cathedral.

In addition to his inspirational radio and television programs, such as the 1957 series on the life of Christ entitled *Quo Vadis America*, Sheen wrote numerous books — sixty-six in all — and used the sales to support foreign missions. He covered a vast array of topics in his books like he did on television and radio, including theology, science, morality, marriage, priesthood, and philosophy. Perhaps his most popular was *Life of Christ*, in print for more than fifty years. Bishop Sheen's personal love and devotion to the Mother of God were on full display with his written works, with three published books with the Blessed Virgin Mary as the subject, and all are formally and uniquely dedicated to her.

He became the national director of the New York-based Society for the Propagation of the Faith in 1958, a long-held position supervising 129 diocesan directors throughout the country that he relished for years as his favorite role, where was able to visit the missions in Africa and other parts of the world. He was able to effectively raise awareness and funds. In 1966, he was named bishop of Rochester by Pope Paul VI as he continued his work on a new television show, *The Fulton Sheen Program*, that lasted until 1968.

Sheen retired in 1969 at the age of seventy-four and returned to New York City to teach and lead retreats. That same year, he was named titular Archbishop of Newport, Wales. His most treasured accolade came near the end of his life, when on October 2, 1979, Pope John Paul II, during his visit to St. Patrick's Cathedral in New York City, embraced the weakened archbishop with the words, "You have written and spoken well of the Lord Jesus Christ. You are a loyal son of the Church." Archbishop Fulton J. Sheen died two months later, on December 9, 1979, at the age of eighty-four.

The Peoria Diocese opened the cause for Sheen's canonization in 2002, and in June 2012 his heroic virtues were recognized by Pope Benedict XVI as he was declared venerable. The identification and verification of a miracle is normally a giant hurdle and reason that most sainthood causes stall for decades or even centuries. But in the case of Sheen, the needed medical cure through his intercession came to the fore quickly. A dramatic miraculous healing in September 2010 of James Fulton Engstrom, son of Bonnie and Travis Engstrom of the Peoria-area town of Goodfield, who was apparently stillborn without breath or a heartbeat for sixty-one minutes, was submitted to Rome. It was approved unanimously by the Medical Commission of the Congregation for the Causes of Saints as being without natural explanation, noting that the child had survived without any cognitive or developmental deficit. A long delay would follow, however, until the long-standing legal dispute related to the final resting place of his mortal remains was resolved. Pope Francis then approved, on July 5, 2019, the promulgation of the decree of the miracle, thus clearing the way for his beatification. The saintly archbishop was scheduled to be beatified in Peoria on December 21, 2019, but the ceremony was postponed.

⁀

PRAYER FOR THE CANONIZATION OF VENERABLE FULTON SHEEN

Heavenly Father, source of all holiness, You raise up within the Church in every age men and women who serve with heroic love and dedication. You have blessed Your Church through the life and ministry of Your faithful servant, Archbishop Fulton J. Sheen. He has written and spoken well of Your Divine Son, Jesus Christ, and was a true instrument of the Holy Spirit in touching the hearts of countless people.

If it be according to Your Will, for the honor and glory of the Most Holy Trinity and for the salvation of souls, we ask You to move the Church to proclaim him a saint.

We ask this prayer through Jesus Christ, our Lord. Amen.

Imprimatur: +Most Reverend Daniel R. Jenky, C.S.C.,
Bishop of Peoria

☙

Please report any miracles or favors to:

Archbishop Fulton John Sheen Foundation
419 NE Madison Avenue
Peoria, IL 61603
(309) 671-1550
archbishopsheencause.org
info@sheencause.org

Venerable Celestine Bottego

A Late Vocation ahead of Her Time

> Born: December 20, 1895 (Glendale, Ohio)
> Died: August 20, 1980 (Parma, Italy)
> Venerated:: October 31, 2013 (Pope Francis)

Sr. Rosetta could understand why the other nun was so confused. It was only 1954, after all, and she and Mother Celestine stood out for almost disappearing among the long veils propped up on the starched forms of many of the other religious women in the room. They were all nuns serving in the Diocese of Worcester, Massachusetts, but in simple, contemporary suits, the foundress of the Missionaries of Mary and Sr. Rosetta looked like laypeople.

Glendale

"Do you know that this is a meeting of nuns?" another sister gently asked Sr. Rosetta.

"Yes, yes," she said, with an Italian accent. "We are nuns too."

"Oh," said the other sister, intrigued.

"We're a new congregation of missionaries," Sr. Rosetta launched what turned into an interesting conversation.

Mother Celestine had found plenty of support for the unconventional but intentional habit of the new community.

"I spoke with Bishop Fulton Sheen. He encouraged me and said that he was enthusiastic about the idea of our having a lay habit. He said we are the only congregation of this kind until now. He added, it was about time to change," Mother Celestine wrote to Fr. James Spangolo in Italy.

Though renewal had long been on the mind of the Xaverian Missionary Fathers, Mother Celestine and Fr. Spagnolo weren't trying to change anything. They were simply answering the call of God to bring the gospel to people who had yet to hear to good news. It seemed simpler and more practical to wear plain lay clothes when looking to venture into far-off lands in Africa or Asia.

Perhaps it was also the Yankee-ness of her American citizenship or her upbringing in the Wild West or her mature age that made Mother Celestine more inclined to a practical approach to the religious habit.

Mother Celestine Bottego was the middle child of immigrants Mary Healy and Giambattista Bottego. Her Irish mother and Italian father had met in California. Giambattista then moved to the booming mining town of Butte, Montana, and Mary followed soon after. There they married and settled. Celestine was born in 1895. From her father, she would inherit an Italian estate and the vision of the explorer. Not only had Giambattista left Italy to make his way in the New World, but his brother Vittorio had also become an explorer with the Italian Navy. From her mother, Celestine would inherit an Irish love for literature, a sense of humor, and a calm, endearing demeanor.

"I hope they will grow well, so that they can find happiness in life. Their happiness certainly depends on what their mom taught them before they were born, even if a person can learn a lot through education … to be calm and happy," Giambattista wrote to his wife.

Celestine was obviously growing up in a household where happiness was sought beyond material things. They stood in contrast to much of what they found around them. The Sisters of Charity of Leavenworth had opened a school at St. Patrick's Church in town, but open prostitution continued unabated in the town of copper barons willing to exploit anything and anyone to make a fortune. The spring melt always revealed a few dead bodies behind saloons and beyond the city limits. In 1897, Giambattista's brother had also died during his second expedition into the Horn of Africa. His commitment to family over fortune took Giambattista back to Italy in 1900 to care for his elderly parents. He took with him Celestine's older sister, Maria, and her younger brother, Vittorio. Mary stayed behind with four-year-old Celestine to look after their real estate investments.

The next ten years of Celestine's childhood would be marked by the influence of her mother and the Sisters of Charity of Leavenworth. Mary loved poetry and introduced her daughter to the best in the English language. The two women spent much time in long conversations too.

"I have always considered it a grace to have lived close to my mother. She was a strong and sweet character together; she had a great heart and a deep sense of humor. She also spoke with me of very serious things, we read books in English and memorized the poems she liked most," Celestine later remembered.

Among the sisters at school, Celestine had two favorites—Sr. Mida and Sr. Perfecta. From Sr. Mida she took her Confirmation name, Mida, and to Sr. Perfecta she confided that she wanted to be a nun. The inspiration of a religious vocation had come to her after making a short retreat at the convent. Celestine and Sr. Perfecta would keep up an epistolary friendship for years after Celestine returned to Italy. The future foundress was also an excellent student. In July 1910, Celestine earned the highest score on the state exams among eighth graders in Montana. *The Butte Miner* reported her award-winning grades and captured her bright smile in a photograph, the same smile and clear eyes that would appear in photographs decades later.

In 1910, Celestine and her mother rejoined the rest of the family in Parma, Italy, on the family estate and farm. Celestine played soccer with her brother and continued her education at the University of Parma, studying to become an English teacher. She then started teaching in a local middle school. She also taught catechism in her parish church and was involved in the Red Cross and Catholic Action. She came under the influence, too, of the Benedictine Abbot Emmanuel Caronti, a leader in the liturgical movement of the time. Celestine embraced Benedictine spirituality and became a Benedictine oblate in 1922, when she was twenty-six. Two years later, her sister Maria entered the Congregation of Franciscan Missionaries of Mary and was sent to India. Religious life still tugged at Celestine's heart, too, as she wrote to Sr. Perfecta.

"So your sister has made the sacrifice you contemplated so long. If ever you had a religious vocation, you have it yet. Do not let anything interfere with it, if you value your own happiness. The very fact that you have not married during all the time since you finished school leads me to believe a religious vocation. There is nowhere on earth where you are needed more than right here now," the Irish nun chided and encouraged.

But Celestine also felt a duty to care for her parents, and neither she nor Sr. Perfecta knew where Celestine would be truly needed. For the time being, Celestine poured her heart out in helping those around her and in prayer. Dom Emmanuel had encouraged Celestine to reach out to the poor of Parma. On the outskirts of the city, she found youth without. She turned the bottom floor of the family home into a place where they could find in her a concerned friend and a second home. She also gave them catechism classes and organized other activities to keep them out of trouble.

Celestine also had an exceptional capacity for friendship. Everyone in her neighborhood turned to her for advice and assistance. With her they had "a friendship that makes you remember God's love in you" and found in her "a happy person who radiated confidence, serenity, and whose heart invited you to love Jesus and your brothers."

Though Celestine's mission had a small radius, within her own city a new missionary congregation was growing. The bishop of Ravenna, but a Parma native, St. Guido Conforti, was training and forming the Xaverian Missionary Fathers to take the gospel to remote corners abroad. He had been named bishop of Ravenna at the age of thirty-seven and was a remarkable figure of priestly dignity and humility, admired by fellow saints such as Pope John XXIII. With his missionary mind, he had encouraged Pope Pius XI to open an ecumenical council in Rome to reorient the church around missionary activity and interreligious dialogue, among other renovations. When Celestine met him sometime before his death in 1931, she, too, was impressed. Neither of them knew, though, that she would become the first and founding member of the corresponding women's community he had always wanted to start.

In 1936, at the age of forty, she visited her sister in India and spent a month helping in her mission. She joined her sister on visits to the outposts in small villages, bringing medicine, caring for the sick, and even baptizing. Celestine herself baptized some forty babies during that month. In 1938, she started a new teaching position—English teacher at the seminary of the Xaverian Missionaries. Over the years, she got to know Fr. James Spagnolo, one of the congregation's most influential priests. In 1943, he approached Celestine about starting a women's branch of the Xaverian community. She laughed him off.

"I am more capable of destroying God's work than making it happen," she said.

But she didn't quite feel at peace. From the outside, it looked completely strange that a forty-eight-year-old with no experience of religious life would be suddenly called to found a religious community of missionaries. In fact, that is exactly what Celestine's spiritual director thought. She was not cut out for religious life, let alone the person to undertake the formation of a new community. Still, perhaps the words of Sr. Perfecta, or remembrances of the missions in India, and most certainly the Holy Spirit, kept her thinking about religious life and the missions.

But her personal struggle was momentarily eclipsed by the war raging around her. Her family home had become a refuge for anyone in need, from prisoners of war to bombed-out families. In the midst of the chaos, an Easter card from Fr. Spagnolo reached her. He wanted to drop one more hint. On the front was a copy of Velasquez's crucifixion. Inside he had written a single word, "All." It suddenly hit Celestine. If she wanted to give her all to God, this was what she had to do. She asked for the grace to never go back on her commitment.

"We have a foundress," Fr. Spagnolo wrote in his diary.

In 1945, the Missionaries of Mary began to take shape. Several other women joined Celestine, and they won the approval of the Bishop of Parma. Their initial mission territory was Parma itself, where the Bottego family home had become their convent. Celestine and Fr. Spagnolo consulted with Rome about the sisters' habit and received approval to wear lay clothes. "Let love be your habit," Fr. Spagnolo encouraged the new nuns.

In 1954, they received their first missionary call when the Xaverian Fathers asked the sisters to support their seminary in Massachusetts. Cooking and doing laundry for the seminarians, working only within the seminary, was initially frustrating for Mother Celestine and Sr. Rosetta, especially since they knew that there were so many needs in the world. But Celestine never complained. She stayed with Sr. Rosetta at the seminary for a year before returning to Parma to continue to direct the young community. In Massachusetts, more opportunities for mission work started to present themselves, and the sisters expanded into education and charity, especially among Hispanics. Other foreign missions followed—Brazil in 1957, Japan in 1959, and Burundi in 1961. "Always open arms.... She was a mother. She was writing all the time and asking how the community was," one of the first sisters remembered.

In October 1962, Mother Celestine attended the opening session of the Second Vatican Council. This event, too, she followed closely, welcoming its reforms and teachings. Over the years, the missions grew to include Cameroon, Chad, the Congo, Thailand, and Mexico. Mother Celestine visited her missionary sisters and followed them closely with letters. In 1966, the Xaverian Missionaries of Mary convened their first general chapter. To everyone's surprise, Mother Celestine resigned her position as superior, preferring to leave room for younger members and to accompany her sisters by prayer.

"You can well understand as time goes on, how our work demands ever new and fresh energy and youthful gifts to respond to new challenges. Our work is moving forward, and it cannot slow its pace. I wish to withdraw, better observe and follow the activity of all of you, my daughters, and proffer spiritual assistance," she wrote in her resignation letter.

She remained close to her sisters all over the world through her copious letters.

"I have many of your letters here that keep me in close union with each of you and keep me updated on all the activities.... In May there is Mother's Day. I will celebrate all your mothers asking for the consolations that every mother wants, that is, that their children manage to assert themselves in life, according to their vocation, that they know how to bring a little light, joy and truth, honoring their family wherever they are called to live," she wrote to them in May 1969.

Her spiritual guidance from the background would continue for another decade.

In 1977, she was diagnosed with breast cancer. She died on August 20, 1980.

"Her eyes — they were brilliant," one of her sisters recalled. "So much light was coming from them.... Mother was always serene, with a smile, and deep faith in God's will."

She was declared venerable in 2013.

☞

PRAYER FOR THE INTERCESSION OF
VENERABLE CELESTINE BOTTEGO

Almighty and merciful God, you placed in the heart of
Mother Celestina Healy Bottego the burning desire that your

kingdom be extended to the ends of the earth. You enabled
her to give her all for the birth of a missionary family. We
ask you to glorify her on earth and, through her intercession,
to grant us the grace we seek in faith.

Father, may your kingdom come soon through Mary!
Our Father, Hail Mary, Glory Be

☞

Please report any miracles or favors to:

Xaverian Missionaries of Mary
242 Salisbury Street
Worcester, MA 01609
(508) 757-0514
XaverianMissionaries.org

Venerable Mary Angeline Teresa McCrory
Kinder Than Kindness Itself

Born: January 21, 1893 (Brockagh, Ireland)
Died: January 21, 1984 (Germantown, New York)
Venerated: June 28, 2012 (Pope Benedict XVI)

It was fitting for Mother Angeline McCrory to live to be ninety-one years old and die surrounded by the love and care of her spiritual daughters. She had founded the Carmelites of the Aged and Infirm to care for the elderly. She was just receiving the same kindness she had always shown to others.

Mother Angeline was born in Ireland in 1893. She was baptized Brigid Teresa McCrory by her parents Thomas and Brigid McCrory. Her early years were spent on the family farm, and she grew up close to her maternal grandfather. When she was seven, the McCrorys moved to Carfin, Scotland, in search of better job prospects. Brigid was also the second of the five McCrory children and the ringleader of their play.

Germantown ★

One afternoon, her mother looked up from her housework to see her daughter eye to eye with her on the other side of the window. Little Brigid was trying out a neighbor's stilts and thought she would surprise her mother. But she also had a shy, serious, and pious side. As she got older, she often stopped in Holy Family Church near the McCrory home to pray and helped the pastor, Fr. Dean Croonan, arrange the flowers to decorate the altar for feast days. He saw a religious vocation in Brigid and the seeds of holiness.

She, too, was thinking of entering the convent. She had been attending the Elmwood Convent School since she was twelve. French was her favorite subject. She even started using the French spelling of her name. When she met the French nuns, the Little Sisters of the Poor, she wasn't deterred by having to make her novitiate in France. The sisters dedicated themselves to caring for the elderly poor and begged to support themselves and those they cared for. Brigid had met them as they came through town begging. In 1911, her father died tragically in an accident at the steel mill where he worked. Nevertheless, the following year, Brigid decided to enter the Little Sisters of the Poor.

On her way to the train station, she stopped by the rectory to say goodbye to Fr. Croonan. As a farewell gift, he offered her any book she wanted from his library. She closed her eyes and picked. When she looked at the title, she saw she had chosen a biography of St. Teresa of Ávila. She then got on the train to Glasgow, where she would start her life with the Little Sisters of the Poor, and ate a whole box of chocolates to assuage the pain of leaving home. After a short postulancy in Scotland, she went on to France, first to Paris to improve her French and then to La Tour for her novitiate. She took the religious name "Sr. Angeline of St. Agatha." In 1915, she professed her first vows.

The First World War was raging, delaying her departure for her first assignment: Brooklyn, New York. In the meantime, she helped care for wounded soldiers in La Tour until there was a ship ready to brave the German submarines menacing the Atlantic. The next eight years she spent at St. Augustine's Home in Brooklyn. In 1924, she returned to France to prepare to make her final vows. After her profession, she was sent back to America. She served in Pittsburgh for a short time and was then appointed superior of the convent and nursing home in the Bronx.

It was 1926, and over the years the now-Mother Angeline had come to realize that the French customs that structured how the Little Sisters of the Poor cared for the elderly didn't always best serve the aged in America. As superior in the Bronx, she implemented changes she thought made the American elderly more comfortable. She created a more middle-class homelike environment and celebrated American holidays with the residents. She encouraged their independence and freedom and permitted married couples to remain living together in the same room if they wished. Her innovations came to an end when the Mother General of the order came for visitation. The international community was still trying to consolidate and recover unity after the Great War. The Little Sisters of the Poor were not ready for innovations at that point in time. During her annual retreat, Mother Angeline still felt a strong call to serve the elderly in a new way, a way that it didn't seem would be possible in her current circumstances.

She felt American culture, expectations, and tastes needed to be accommodated. She had also realized that the middle class, not just the poor, often needed someone to care for them in old age. She approached Cardinal Patrick Hayes of New York with her ideas and asked for advice. He, too, thought that more needed to be done for the elderly. He encouraged her to strike out on a new path. If it were God's will, she would succeed, he told her. This gave her the courage to move forward. In 1929, she and six other sisters received a dispensation from Rome to leave the Little Sisters of the Poor.

The founding sisters of the Carmelites of the Aged and Infirm stayed temporarily with the Sparkill Dominicans. The teaching sisters helped Mother Angeline and the other sisters sew their new brown habits. Mother Angeline's Carmelite soul was coming out, and the Carmelite Friars had taken an interest in her project from the beginning. The new community would be Carmelite. She was given an empty rectory in Upper Manhattan to start with. In September 1929, she opened the St. Martin of Tours Home with seven residents. In 1931, the new community became officially affiliated with the Order of Carmel.

Mother Angeline was ahead of her time and faced criticism for her approach to elder care. She got rid of the constrained, institutional feel more typical of the time in favor of a cozier, warmer atmosphere. She also included rehabilitation care in the services and more opportunities for recreation and entertainment. With time, the emerging science of gerontology would vindicate her instincts and silence her critics. The Great Depression was also settling over the country as she was opening the first convent. But nothing deterred her. On the contrary, the community grew quickly, and she opened homes at lightning speed.

In 1932, she made a visit to her family in Scotland. It brought back memories to the foundress as much as her presence aroused the interest of her old neighbors. "I went to make an evening visit to the parish church and I found it so much smaller than I pictured it as a child. I kneeled on the bench of my childhood days and knelt for a few minutes," she wrote in a letter to her community. "Everyone in the parish seemed to know that I was home, for the next morning after Mass, crowds of old-timers stood around in front of the church waiting to shake my hands and cry over me. For a moment, I wished I was back in New York as it was all very embarrassing."

Kindness was one of her outstanding virtues. She always showed the volunteers at the nursing homes her gratitude and often had little gifts for them. For the novices, too, she also had a little something, usually fresh donuts. She loved the elderly, but the youth of the newest members of the community energized her. She often said that she never wanted to live in a house without novices, and she never did. She taught her sisters to give the elderly tender and affectionate care. "If you must fail, fail on the side of kindness. Be kinder than kindness itself to the old people." she would say. The theme of kindness appears time and again in her pieces of advice to her sisters. "Efficiency is wonderful, but it should never replace kindness"; and, "the best remedy for any elderly person is still TLC"; and, "I entreat you be kind, be patient, and be always understanding. Begin with yourself" were some of her most remembered maxims.

Her Irish sense of humor stayed with her even after decades in America. Early in the community's history, she had a meeting with a young woman who was considering entering. Actually, the girl was so undecided that she had not wanted to keep the appointment, but her mother made her come along with her. Mother Angeline found them both waiting for her when she opened her office door.

"Well, which one of you wants to enter?" she said as a greeting.

Mother Angeline's warmth and humor convinced the young woman that her vocation was to the Carmelites of the Aged and Infirm.

With laughter went music. Mother Angeline loved inviting often visiting clergy, from cardinals to ordinary priests, to the convent. She often turned these meetings into parties with the sisters playing and singing music. She had a special love for clergy. After she died, the sisters found she had written the following:

> Sometimes remembering what my Patroness, St. Teresa, said that when we feel we are so near to the King, we should make our petitions to Him, I always plead for souls. First, for Priests, that they may reach the height of sanctity to which their vocation calls them. I entered religion chiefly with the intention of sacrificing myself for Priests, realizing how God must delight in the soul of a Priest, and its immense influence over the salvation of other souls. I have always kept this object of my religious life in view, and I feel confident I can help my brother Priests, especially by my prayers and penances for their intentions.

She was friends with many of the most influential churchmen of her time, but she hobnobbed with cardinals with the naturalness that comes with humility. The honor she paid them came from saw seeing Christ in them.

In 1957, the Carmelites of the Aged and Infirm received official approval as a religious congregation. On the heels of this approval followed the Second Vatican Council. She embraced the teachings of the Second Vatican Council and the changing times she lived in. Responding to the needs of the time was at the core of her work.

"Vatican II has shown the religious her place in the church and is asking us to meet the challenge of the times and the spirit of the gospels and in imitation of Christ," she addressed her sisters in the 1960s:

I ask that you dedicate yourselves to Christ, promising him that you will be faithful to him and will value the divine call of your precious gift of a religious vocation. Christ is the same yesterday today and forever and when the world is changing about us, He is our constant guide, the way, the truth and the life. Our congregation was founded 39 years ago and under much criticism. We introduced many of the changes that are just going into effect today in a number of religious communities. Our goal was to provide up-to-date home life here for the aged because this is the work entrusted to us by the church. We wanted always to measure up to the highest standards and we have always endeavored to keep up with the progress of the times.

Mother Angeline was herself hard to keep up with. When she celebrated her Golden Jubilee as a religious and thirty years since the founding of the Carmelites of the Aged and Infirm, she had opened forty nursing homes. The count would reach fifty-nine by the time she died. For her work in advancing elder care and the mission of the Church, she was awarded the *Pro Ecclesia et Pontifice* Award in 1965, the National Award of Honor from the American Association of Homes for Aging in 1969, honorary degrees in Doctor of Humane Letters from Siena College and Manhattan College in 1970, and the *Papal Benemerenti* Award in 1978.

Her life was now advancing into old age. In 1978, she stepped down as the community's top leader. Her bond with her sisters in religion grew deeper and tenderer. As she declined and needed more and more of the care she had given to others, she accepted it amiably. Even as she grew quite frail, she still loved to gather the sisters together and sing, and sometimes she directed too.

In January 1984, she suddenly took a turn for the worse. She died surrounded by her sisters on January 21. She was declared venerable in 2012.

❦

PRAYER FOR THE INTERCESSION OF
VENERABLE MARY ANGELINE TERESA McCRORY

Almighty and eternal Father, we thank You for the inspiration You gave to Your daughter, Mother M. Angeline Teresa, to establish the Carmelite Sisters for the Aged and Infirm, and to provide loving care for countless elderly men and women with compassion and a respect for their dignity and a regard for life in all its stages. If it be Your gracious will, grant that the virtues of Mother M. Angeline Teresa may be recognized and provide a lasting example for Your people. We ask this through Our Lord Jesus Christ, Your Son, Who lives and reigns with You and the Holy Spirit, One God, forever and ever. Amen.

❦

Please report any miracles or favors to:

Office of the Vice-Postulator
c/o Carmelite Sisters for the Aged and Infirm
600 Woods Road
Germantown, NY 12526
(518) 537-5000
MotherAngeline.org

Venerable Alphonse Gallegos, Bishop
Bishop of the Barrio

Born: February 20, 1931 (Albuquerque, NM)
Died: October 6, 1991 (Sacramento, CA)
Venerated: July 8, 2016 (Pope Francis)

The new auxiliary bishop was never in his office. He had, as one journalist put it, "taken it to the streets." As he had in southern California, he walked the streets of Sacramento's Hispanic neighborhoods, talking with youth and visiting families. On Friday and Saturday nights, he always stopped by the gatherings of "low riders" hanging around street corners. He admired their mechanical skills used to trick out their cars, encouraged them to put those talents to good use, blessed their automobiles, and invited them to church. And he did it all with a genuine warmth and a smile.

Bishop Alphonse Gallegos got the nickname "Bishop of the Barrio."

He had himself grown up in a *barrio*, the Spanish word for neighborhood, often applied to Hispanic parts of American cities. His family was originally from Albuquerque, New Mexico, and was part of the area's Hispanic culture, with roots reaching back to when the state was part of the Spanish Empire. Their faith was deep too. At home, they had daily catechism classes after finishing their homework and prayed the Rosary after dinner. Alphonse's father was a carpenter, and the Gallegos took St. Joseph as their patron. Every year on his feast, they threw a huge party for the neighbors.

Alphonse had been born with severe myopia. To get better treatment for him and more opportunities for his ten siblings, the Gallegos family moved to Watts, California, outside of Los Angeles. The town also had colonial roots, and by the 1930s, it had become a transport hub for the railroad and a melting pot of ethnicities and immigrants. Alphonse attended public school, where he could take special classes. As he got older, he became an altar server and took private Latin courses with the Augustinian Recollects at their parish, St. Michael's Church. He wanted to be a priest. At sixteen, he had eye surgery that significantly improved his vision, at least temporarily, so that he was able to graduate from a regular high school. In 1950, he entered the Augustinian Recollects and went to Kansas City, Missouri, for his novitiate. He made his first vows in 1951 and his final vows in 1954.

His eyesight had held out through his novitiate and undergraduate studies at Rockhurst University, but during his seminary years at the Tagaste Monastery in Suffern, New York, his retina started to dystrophy. Surgery saved the vision in his right eye, but he could see little with his left eye. His poor vision made academics difficult for him, despite his dedication. The breviary, too, became so hard for him to read that he was given a dispensation to say the Rosary during community prayers. His superiors doubted whether they could let him be ordained. Their first decision was to ordain him and require him to take a few more years of classes before letting him hear confessions. But some of the monks questioned the legitimacy of such an exemption. The next vote was a stalemate — four in favor and four against. The decision rested in the hands of the abbot. Br. Alphonse's humility and generosity got him to the altar. He was ordained in 1958 and given full faculties.

His superiors didn't want to overburden him, and so he was first given various chaplaincies — a convent, a hospital, a summer camp for the visually impaired. He was a kind of priest-greeter at the monastery, beloved for his kindness, gentleness, and sense of humor. He never complained, neither about his work nor his condition. He started to learn Braille and also learned to drive, though this prospect terrified his community. At the same time, he requested to continue his education. He first studied psychology at Thomas Aquinas University in Sparkill, attending night classes, and then went on earn a master's in urban education from John's University in Jamaica, New York.

In 1966, he was sent to Kansas City to take over as novice master. This position tested his patience. The new generation was more individualistic and self-conscious. It was a time of change in both Church and society, but they questioned everything in a way that was foreign to a man more humble and obedient, even though Fr. Alphonse certainly embraced the changes of Vatican II. But his novices found him fair, if strict, prayerful, and always cheerful. In his boundless optimism, every day was "a beautiful morning" for Fr. Alphonse.

Meanwhile, his hometown had become the epicenter of the race riots of the 1960s. The prior recorded in the monastery journal that things were "out of control in Watts, the central section of the district is in flames." Violent crime—vandalism, burglary, daytime muggings, gang activity—became rampant. Those with a middle-class income moved out, leaving the poor and the riffraff behind. No one went out at night. The pastor at St. Michael's was grateful that the few who attended Christmas midnight Mass made it to church and back home without incident. In 1972, Fr. Alphonse, usually called Fr. Al, was reassigned to his childhood parish. He objected that, as the Bible warned, he would have little chance of being accepted by his own, but he obeyed.

His fears proved completely unfounded. His warm personality and genuine humility completely won the community over to its native son. As pastor, he made education the pillar of his strategy for the parish. The parish had a school, but he knew that, with most of his parishioners living below the poverty line, it needed additional financial support. He moved his contacts from Watts to Hollywood and brought the enrollment up to 350 students. He was there, too, every morning to greet the students and to see them off in the afternoon. He modeled his vision of the deeper purpose of Catholic education for the teachers and administrators. He wanted all the students to leave St. Michael's with a deep sense of their dignity as human persons, pride in their cultural heritage, and authentic relationships with God.

For older youth, he revitalized the Catholic Youth Organization and created additional programs to engage and form them. Teens who had before vandalized the parish buildings with graffiti were invited to paint thoughtful murals. Former gang members became tutors in the adult education program. He also initiated rounds of home visits, often simply having dinner with his parishioners. He was easy to be with, and children loved him, so he was always a welcome guest. It was here that he started his famous walks through the neighborhood and first became "the chaplain of the low riders." As he told a reporter, "During my six years at Watts, I visited the youth in their homes, met with them on street corners and the basketball court, invited them to the rectory, had programs for them in the parish hall, and took them to colleges and universities. We saw twenty-seven young men and women graduate from college. Before, standing on the street corner, they felt the world had nothing to offer ... until they discovered that they had something to offer the world."

Though he had a special love for youth and a natural link with Hispanics, he sought out and included everyone in the diverse community. His birthday became an annual multicultural potluck with the various ethnic groups he worked with. He also started a parish Thanksgiving dinner that gathered three to four hundred people in the church hall for the traditional turkey and stuffing. One evening, he was seen lifting an intoxicated man from the street and carrying him to the rectory. The priest took care of him until he sobered up and could safely walk home.

When he left St. Michael's in 1978 to take up a new parish assignment, the parish council noted that he had singlehandedly revitalized their community. Watts may have still been poor, but it had new life. At his new parish, he also quickly won the hearts of the faithful, but his time at Cristo Rey in Glendale was limited. In 1979, he was asked to become the director of the newly created Hispanic Affairs Office of the California Catholic Conference. He placed himself at the disposition of his superiors. They would miss his presence in the monastic community, but they told him to accept the position.

Still wanting to be close to parish life and ministry, he re-sided at a parish in another *barrio*. But his pastoral wandering now had a wider circumference, as he met with Church and civic leaders across the state. His first concern was the spiritual state of the many new Hispanic immigrants who had left the more Catholic milieu of their homelands. To provide education and catechesis, he started a Spanish language radio station and trained a network of catechists. He also took up the labor question and immigration, even internationally. At the invitation of the Secretariat for Hispanic Affairs of the National Conference of Catholic Bishops, he spoke at a meeting on Church and labor in Caracas, Venezuela.

His work for the California Catholic Conference caught the attention of members of the hierarchy. On August 21, 1981, Bishop Quinn asked Fr. Alphonse to meet him at the corner of Eleventh and First Streets. The future bishop recorded what happened in his journal.

> I met the bishop at 5:15 pm and he immediately told me that His Holiness Pope John Paul II had nominated me to the Episcopacy. I felt humbled and stunned. We talked for a few minutes. I frankly asked the Bishop if he really wanted me to serve as his Auxiliary Bishop. He answered that he would be delighted if I would accept. I asked if I could pray over this serious appointment. He allowed me to spend the night in prayer and asked me to call him at 8:30 the next morning. I spent the night in prayer asking the Holy Spirit to enlighten me to make the right decision and to do the will of God. I asked our Lady to assist me to be humble and open to the will of her Son. I felt frightened and humbled. My nomination as auxiliary Bishop of Sacramento and Titular Bishop of Sasabe was a complete surprise to me.

Aug. 22 I called Bishop Francis Quinn to give him my answer. I shared his advice: "the Holy Spirit had chosen you." I never felt the presence of the Holy Spirit as I did this day. For Holy Obedience to our Holy Father and strengthened by the Holy Spirit, I accepted to become Auxiliary Bishop of Sacramento and Titular Bishop of Sasabe. Once I responded to the will of God, a calm came over me. I then went to celebrate the Eucharist in thanksgiving and personal dedication to God and His Church.

As auxiliary bishop, he was given charge of the Hispanic ministry in the diocese. He continued many of the activities that had characterized his years as pastor and his work at the California Catholic Conference, including his walks around the *barrios* and his visits with low riders. He was rarely seen at the chancery, as he was always visiting someone, whether a simple member of the diocese or a civic leader whose ear he was bending. He seemed to have a hand in everything. He fundraised for a little girl in Peru who needed a liver transplant, launched a campaign to help illegal immigrants apply for legal status when the requirements were loosened, and advocated for bilingual education. He marched with Cesar Chavez and the United Farm Workers and maintained an ongoing friendship with the Hispanic labor leader. He joined the protests to stop the shipment of atomic warheads to the Trident submarine base and joined pro-life demonstrations. He gave two annual day-long retreats at the Folsom Prison.

His concerns had a wide span, but he spent a lot of time in the migrant worker camps. He would say Mass outdoors for the workers and their families, gathering the children close to the altar. He visited with these workers without a permanent home and organized catechesis in preparation for the sacraments. This would lead to the mobile pastoral teams that continued their work after his death.

"I make it a point to be on the ranches and the farms to make the people know by our presence that we are one church," he explained once to a journalist.

He was equally concerned about their temporal conditions and their just treatment.

"We in the United States can better appreciate the work of the undocumented, which is mainly agricultural by thanking God for the food we have on our table ... the fruit and vegetables ... because we ourselves do not want to get into that kind of laborious work," he said in another interview.

His eyesight had deteriorated so that he could only read large print up close. But he never complained, never even mentioned his condition to his secretary. His pastoral ministry marched on.

October 6, 1991, was busy day for him. The night before, he had spoken at the annual deacons' dinner in Roseville, imploring the men and their wives to speak out in defense of life at all stages and in all situations. In the morning, he stood with Catholics and other Christians at the Capital Life Chain praying the Rosary. He held a sign that read "God forgives and heals." He then went to the hospital to visit a young man dying of AIDS. That evening, he had a Confirmation outside of Sacramento in Gridley.

He and his driver were on their way back to Sacramento, coming over the top of a hill, when the car suddenly slowed to a stop. The bishop got out to push the car off the road. The driver coming around the hill couldn't see the bishop until it was too late. She hit him, sending him a hundred feet down the road. He died instantly.

At his funeral, some three hundred low riders helped form one of the longest funeral processions Sacramento had ever seen.

Bishop Alphonse Gallegos was declared venerable in 2016.

⁀

PRAYER FOR THE INTERCESSION OF
VENERABLE ALPHONSE GALLEGOS, O.A.R.

*God our Father, in Bishop Alphonse Gallegos, O.A.R.,
You gave light to Your faithful people. You made him a
pastor of the Church to feed Your sheep with his words and
to teach them by example. We pray that his life of holiness
and service to the People of God be acknowledged and that
this loyal son of Our Lady of Guadalupe be counted among
the saints of Your Kingdom. We ask this blessing through
Christ our Lord. Amen.*

⁀

Please report any miracles or favors to:

Augustinian Recollects
1022 W. Cleveland Avenue
Montebello, CA 90640
https://BishopGallegos.org/
FrEliseo@bishopGallegos.org

Venerable Patrick Peyton
The Rosary Priest

Born: January 9, 1909 (Attymass, Ireland)
Died: June 3, 1992 (San Pedro, California)
Venerated: December 18, 2017 (Pope Francis)

Staring his own mortality in the face and struggling beneath the weight of a terminal diagnosis of tuberculosis on the upper lobe of his right lung, Patrick Peyton sat up on his deathbed, feeling his faith ablaze like a pile of hay sprinkled with gasoline and ignited with a match. The words he had just received from one of his professors, Fr. Cornelius Hagerty, C.S.C., while visiting his hospital room, were the most powerful he had ever heard in his life, and they changed everything:

If you believe twenty-five percent, that's what you will receive. Fifty — that's what you'll get. But if you believe one hundred percent and you give it all to Mary

★ Hollywood

to give to her son, Jesus, to be healed, that is what you'll receive.

Patrick, who at the time was receiving his formation to become a Holy Cross priest, mentally and physically had been at his worst with his condition. He was depressed and had even thought that he had lost his faith. But with those words, he invited his family and friends and fellow seminarians, anybody he could think of, to pray for healing through the intercession of Mary. Fr. Hagerty had reminded him: "What she asks for and insists on she obtains. She has never failed anyone who had recourse to her with faith and perseverance." If he were to be healed, he made a promise to God that he would dedicate his life and his ministry as a priest to devotion to Mary through the family Rosary. Patrick did what his former mentor suggested and prayed to the Virgin Mary for a healing, and on October 31, 1939, he believed to have felt that the cure had taken place. Day by day, he began to get a little stronger. Eventually, the doctors examined the x-rays and told him that he was going to live, but they could not explain how it had happened. Patrick knew that it was Mary who had saved him:

> When I needed her and her power and her friendship, she didn't forget that ever since I had been a little child and could open my mouth, I had used that power to say the Rosary; so when I needed her friendship, she was glad to give it to me.

With a new lease on life, Patrick finished up his studies and became a priest with a mission to spread the Rosary, a devotion that was instilled in him as a young child. He was born in 1909, the sixth of nine children, to a very poor farming family in County Mayo, Ireland. His mother and father, when they got married, decided that they were going to be a Rosary family, so they would pray it each night after dinner. Witnessing his father John's "Spirit of faith," getting down on his knees to lead the family in prayer each night, made a big impact on Patrick. He would later reflect that his family was the great blessing of his life because it became all he needed—a home, a library, a university—where he learned all of the essential elements of the Faith. He started to see what the prayers meant and how the mysteries applied to his life. Devotion to the Rosary was so natural to him that on one occasion when young Patrick was visiting a nearby village farm where they needed help picking potatoes, he was surprised when that family did not pray the Rosary after dinner like his had done on every day of his life. So he decided then with bold faith to explain the value and meaning of the Rosary to the farmer and encouraged him to lead his family in prayer.

Even as a young man, Patrick had a great desire to become a priest, perhaps beginning at the age of nine when one of his friends, John Barrett, arranged for him the high honor of serving Mass at his home parish, St. Joseph in Attymass. Over the course of his teenage years, he would attend many retreats and talks there. His dream later grew into a plan to study for the priesthood and become a missionary, so Patrick began to write letters to missionary societies. The Redemptorists in Italy were the first to suggest the priesthood to Patrick, but nothing came of it. The Capuchins, also in Italy, appealed to him, and he believed that it was the community for him, but he never heard from them and felt dejected. At the suggestion of his parish priest, he then tried to get a scholarship from the Society of African Missionaries—but he was refused again: "We are sorry ... but Patrick is not up to the required standard in mathematics."

With those rejections, Patrick began to seriously doubt his "foolish dream" of becoming a priest. He had abandoned his plans by 1927, at which point he decided to come to the United States to try to become a millionaire selling real estate. He thought to join his three sisters and relatives who had settled in Scranton, Pennsylvania. As excited as he was to try out this new American adventure, getting his father's consent would not be easy. There was one condition to be met before Patrick and his brother, Tom, left for America to live with their sister Nellie. His father commanded them to go down on their knees and make a promise before the icon of the Sacred Heart always to be faithful in America to the Lord.

After he and his brother arrived in America, he searched for weeks without success for employment. Nellie set up a meeting with Msgr. Kelly, which Patrick declined, but the priest persisted and offered him a job as a sexton (janitor) in the cathedral, which was eventually accepted. It was during that time working in silence and prayer that Patrick's dream of becoming a missionary priest reemerged. With his desire for the priesthood reignited, but still needing to resolve the issue of his education, Patrick began his freshman year of high school at the age of nineteen at St. Thomas High School in Scranton.

In the spring of 1929, a band of Holy Cross Fathers passed through his area and gave a mission that he attended. During this time, he approached Fr. Pat Dolan, a priest of the Congregation of Holy Cross, and said "I want to join Holy Cross." Perhaps he felt a connection or familiarity of a sort to his upbringing in Ireland, but he later reflected that he was attracted to their family atmosphere, charism to assist diocesan clergy, and obedience. He was accepted with the help of Msgr. Kelly's strong letter of recommendation: "I envy the community or the bishop that finally gets him."

Both he and his brother quickly were off to the Holy Cross Minor Seminary at the University of Notre Dame for their priestly formation. There Patrick felt that he had found a second family, who also prayed the Rosary as part of their daily routine. He knew that this was where God wanted him to be. In 1932, the brothers graduated and began their novitiate. This was an intensive year of spiritual exercises that included living with and learning about the Congregation of Holy Cross. They professed their temporary vows in 1933 with the Holy Cross and started studying for bachelor of arts degrees at the University of Notre Dame, which they completed in 1937, followed by further theological training at Holy Cross College at the Catholic University of America in Washington, D.C. There, Patrick's dream to be a missionary continued to take shape as he lived in the Bengalese house with other seminarians with similar aspirations.

Following the miraculous cure from tuberculosis, Patrick felt reinvigorated to continue on his journey to become a priest and to dedicate his life to the Blessed Virgin Mary through the Rosary: "I gave my heart and soul in love to Mary." He was ordained two years later on June 15, 1941 (the same day as his brother) at Sacred Heart Church at Notre Dame and was given a post as the chaplain to the Holy Cross Brothers in Albany, New York, at the Vincentian Institute.

In his first years there, Fr. Peyton desperately wanted to find a way to thank the Virgin Mary for his miracle, and on retreat one day, he was inspired to conceive of Family Rosary Crusade to try to reach people to encourage them to pray the Rosary, as he was convinced that his healing was given so that he might increase devotion to her. "The family that prays together stays together" was the famous quote of Fr. Peyton that truly began to resonate with families around the world. Peyton began with the help of volunteer students and brothers and sisters from the Vincentian Institute to assist him in writing thousands of letters, including to bishops and cardinals. The first rally in 1948 in London, Ontario grew from a proposed parish mission to a successful rally with over eighty thousand families, including 95 percent of the diocese, in attendance. After holding rallies in the United States, Fr. Peyton set out on a quest to bring the events to 10 million families worldwide: in Latin America (Colombia and Brazil), 4.5 million people attended; in Europe (England, Ireland, and Spain), almost 3.7 million; in Africa (Tanzania, Uganda, Kenya, and South Africa), almost half a million, and in Asia (the Philippines, Thailand, and Singapore), 2.2 million people were in attendance. All told, Fr. Patrick Peyton was seen live by more than 28 million people—more than anyone else in the history of the world before the pontificate of Pope St. John Paul II. Fr. Peyton believed with his whole heart that this particular prayer would indeed be the vehicle through which we could bring greater wholeness to the Church and impact the peoples of the world.

Fr. Patrick Peyton soon realized that to reach as many people as possible he would need to make use of mass media to spread the message. At first, he got a small show on a local radio station in Albany, New York, and it was wildly successful. That gave him the bug, and Fr. Peyton knew if he wanted to reach millions with the family Rosary prayer he had to be on the national level, so he went off to New York City. There he persuaded a non-Christian woman from the Mutual Broadcasting System to give him airtime if he could come up with a big Hollywood star to be on his radio show. He asked "who's the most popular actor in Hollywood today?" Learning that it was Bing Crosby, Fr. Peyton cold called the actor at his house in Beverly Hills. Bing Crosby agreed to be the first guest, and the show was off and running. On May 13, 1945,

Cardinal Spellman came on and introduced the program, and even the new president of the United States, Harry S. Truman, gave an endorsement. Fr. Peyton asked families to pray for peace by saying the Rosary together. It was a huge success: it drew the largest audience that any program on the Mutual Broadcasting System had then experienced.

He knew he needed to go to where the stars were and where the production was happening, so next he headed off to Hollywood. Fr. Peyton identified one of the local parishes where many celebrities worshiped and, one by one, he just asked, "Would you be on my radio show?" By February of 1947, The Family Theater Productions was launched, and he had a national radio show. Quickly, every major Hollywood star, believer and non-believer alike, was inquiring to be on the radio program. Loretta Young, Grace Kelly, Gregory Peck, Jimmy Stewart, Lucille Ball, and Raymond Burr were amongst the A-list Hollywood actors he enlisted.

He was very intuitive in seeing that mass media—first radio and then television and films—could spread the gospel. With the television becoming a fixture in American households in the 1950s, Peyton ventured into content for the screen as early as 1951 with *Hill Number One*, which gave James Dean his first onscreen credits as an actor. He discovered the power of film to bring his Marian devotion to life visually and raised the funds, assembled a team of producers and writers, and shot in Spain on location the fifteen mysteries of the Rosary. This project became a vehicle for evangelization in Latin America to be able to provide a pictorial of the scenes from the life of Christ. He sent huge crates with projectors, film reels, and generators all around the world and, for some people, those films were the very first that they ever saw.

The impact that "the Rosary Priest" had was immense, and even in death he is positioned as a saintly ambassador for family prayer. Peyton's worldwide Rosary Rallies and his far-reaching media work all stemmed from a childhood devotion and making good on a promise made to the Virgin Mary to make her known and loved to millions around the globe.

Fr. Patrick Peyton died on June 3, 1992, and his sainthood cause was opened almost a decade later in 2001. He was declared venerable in 2017.

⁐

PRAYER FOR THE INTERCESSION OF VENERABLE PATRICK PEYTON

God, Our Father, Your wisdom is displayed in all creation, and the power of Your grace is revealed in the lives of holy people who inspire us to trust You more fully and to serve others more generously. In a unique way, You blessed the life and work of Your servant, Fr. Patrick Peyton, C.S.C., and made him a fervent apostle of Mary, Queen of the Holy Rosary and Mother of us all. Through his intercession, we ask for this favor (make your request). Please grant it, if it is for Your honor and glory, through Christ Our Lord. Amen.

⁐

Please report any miracles or favors to:

Holy Cross Family Ministries
518 Washington Street
N. Easton, MA 02356-1200
(508) 238-4095
Fatherpeyton.org
VicePostulator@hcfm.org

Venerable Aloysius Schwartz
Missionary to the Children of the World

Born: September 18, 1930 (Washington, D.C.)
Died: March 16, 1992 (Manila, Philippines)
Venerated: January 22, 2015 (Pope Francis)

Aloysius Schwartz was over halfway through seminary, but it wasn't going fast enough.

"Has the date been set for your wedding?" he wrote to his sister Dolores. "When you talk about not being able to wait, I know just how you feel. Since the fourth grade in grammar school, I have been waiting to leave for the missions. And the older I get, the more intense becomes this desire. It's only natural, but we learn so much by patience. It purifies everything in our selfish hearts and leaves us clean before God."

Perhaps he had first felt a missionary vocation while reading *Boy Commandos*, a comic book series about young heroes who went around the world helping the

Washington, DC

poor. It was his favorite, sent to him and his siblings by an uncle who lived in Montana. Al was the third of the seven Schwartz children, born on September 18, 1930, in Washington, D.C. If not wealthy, the family was close, happy, and sincerely pious. Al had always said he wanted to be a priest when he grew up, so he turned down a scholarship to the local Jesuit high school and instead joined his brother Lou at the minor seminary. Afterwards, his eyes on the missions, he joined the Maryknoll Fathers and earned his bachelor's from Maryknoll College.

He enjoyed his years at Maryknoll, but he sometimes thought life there was too comfortable for men preparing to live and work among the poor. During his novitiate year, he also noticed that some of the men were being sent for higher studies and realized he could end up a teacher instead of a foreign missionary. He decided to apply to The Society of the Auxiliaries of the Missions, based in Belgium. It trained seminarians to be secular priests, incardinated into poor, missionary dioceses around the world. He was accepted, and he left for the Catholic University in Louvain, Belgium, just before Christmas 1952. If he had found the Maryknoll seminary too cozy for future missionaries, the mediocre food, old buildings, and damp climate of the Belgium seminary were a better introduction to harder living conditions. Young and dedicated, he didn't realize the toll it was already taking on his health. He was developing digestive problems that would plague him for the rest of his life.

He also had to figure out what to do with himself during the seminary vacations. He couldn't afford the trip across the Atlantic to visit home, so he usually hitchhiked to a monastery where he stayed and worked or joined Abbé Pierre among the "rag pickers" of the Paris suburbs. He wrote plenty of letters to his family, too, keeping up with the life events of his siblings. His connection with his family remained strong throughout his life, especially with his sister Dolores, who was also key in helping to support his mission work.

In his last year of seminary, he was named "senior student," a kind of class president responsible for bringing the concerns of the student body to the rector. He didn't hesitate to lay out to his superior that he thought the seminary lacked a true international spirit and training, pointing out that all important positions of authority were held by French-speaking Belgians. The rector became defensive, but Al insisted. His seminary education ending on that sour note, Al returned to Washington, D.C., where he would be ordained. He was shocked, though, when he got a letter from the rector stating that he had decided not to approve him for ordination. Al took the first ship he could back again to Belgium to see if he could rectify the situation. He pled his case with Bishop Kerkhofs of Liège, showing his excellent grades and that nothing in his records from the seminary precluded his ordination. He convinced the bishop and made it back to Washington, D.C., with a letter of approval and just enough time to make a retreat before being ordained on June 29, 1957.

His chosen mission field was Korea, still in recovery from the war that had divided it into North and South. In Seoul, Fr. Al got his first impression of the poverty gripping the country, the thousands upon thousands who had lost their homes or fled south and now lived in slums on the edge of the city. Among these poor were thousands of orphans. At Fr. Al's final destination, Busan, 250 miles south of Seoul, the situation was much the same as in the capital.

"Keep your little second graders praying for these good people," he wrote his sister Rose, "especially for the multitude of little waifs their age whom one sees roaming the streets trying to keep the inside warm on a very meager diet and also trying to protect themselves from the cold with very thin and insufficient clothes. Ask them to pray especially for priests. There are at least five parishes without priests in this diocese and a priest can station himself anywhere and within a year's time have a thriving parish because so many people wish to enter the Church."

Fr. Al, too, was suffering from the food and the cold winter, though he never complained. He also had to learn the language. He tried to dedicate five hours a day to study, but the demands for his ministry were already strong enough to create a grueling schedule. Two months into his missionary life, he woke up on the cathedral floor with the chalice lying next to him and the carpet stained with the consecrated wine. He had collapsed during Mass. The diagnosis was hepatitis A with intestinal complications. He sought treatment at various clinics in Korea and kept to a strict diet, but after more than a year of "dragging along on one cylinder," he realized the only way to fully recover was to return to the United States. He took back with him extensive photos of the poverty he had witnessed.

Back home in Washington, D.C., he kept working for his mission. The diocese didn't encourage him to fundraise for Busan because it was supporting another mission, so he wrote to parishes and dioceses all over the country, asking to be allowed to make an appeal for the poor Catholics of Korea. Taking the bus, if he didn't hitchhike, he displayed his photographs to accompany his words. The combination proved very persuasive. Then in 1961, he met Gratian Meyer. Both were making a retreat at the Trappist monastery in Berryville, Virginia. Doing the dishes together one evening, the priest told Gratian about Korea and his hope to return. Gratian, it turned out, was a professional fundraiser, and he offered to help Fr. Al form a non-profit and launch a direct mail campaign. After thinking and praying about it, Fr. Al decided to take Gratian up on his offer and formed Korean Relief, Inc. He also brought Bishop Choi from Busan to America for a speaking tour. Financially, it was a smashing success. Bishop Choi would have been happy to keep Fr. Al in America fundraising, but he agreed instead to let him return to Korea.

Just before Christmas 1961, Fr. Al landed back in his beloved mission land. He lived at the bishop's residence, again, studying Korean and helping with the parish. But it wasn't long before his intestinal trouble flared up. He and Bishop Choi decided he needed to move to a parish without a priest, where he could cook for himself. He would have to study Korean on his own, but this seemed the best way to preserve his health and keep him in Korea. Fr. Al left for Songdo, one of the poorest parishes in the diocese.

He found a somewhat chaotic situation at the parish, especially related to the distribution of humanitarian aid. In theory, the food and materials from Catholic Relief Services were given away according to need and regardless of religion. But Fr. Al discovered that about half of the goods were sold to raise money for the parish and most of the rest simply given to parishioners or prospective converts. He got back in touch with his old Korean teacher, Damiano Park, and hired him as his assistant at the parish, a relationship that would last decades. Damiano's first job was to take charge of the distribution of aid to assure it went to those most in need. Fr. Al also found a Benedictine congregation willing to send him three sisters for the parish. He gave them the rectory for a convent and built a shack for himself nearby. For the next three years, he lived just like most of his parishioners—without electricity or running water, cohabitating with rats and insects, and with the dust and smoke from an open charcoal fire hanging in the air. He considered them some of the most blessed years of his life.

In the midst of establishing himself in Songdo, he also had to make a trip to Rome. His fundraising in the United States had provoked the American bishops, and they wrote to Rome to have it stopped. The Congregation for the Propagation of the Faith, which oversaw mission work, ordered Bishop Choi to immediately cease the mailings. Fr. Al had actually always felt a little a hesitant about the fundraising, but at the same time, something inside him told to keep it going for the poor. He went to Rome to defend his fundraising and lay the needs of the Korean church before Cardinal Agagianian, prefect of the Congregation. It was a delicate operation that would make or break his mission work, so he enlisted the intercession of Sr. Gertrude at the Carmelite monastery in Busan. He felt the hand of Providence over the whole trip and came home from Rome with both the cardinal's promise to ignore the complaints of the American bishops and a giant golden ciborium as a token of the cardinal's approval. He wrote to his sister Dolores that it reminded him of the Wimbledon Cup.

Now he could get down to business. In Songdo, he had seen firsthand how inadequate the already existing charities his fundraising supported actually were. At the orphanages, the children hung around listless and half neglected, and the hospitals lacked basic materials. He decided the best course of action was to create his own institutions, but, again, he knew he needed help. He placed an advertisement in the Catholic weekly looking for women who wanted to dedicate their lives to the service of the poor. He recruited twelve. With the help of the Benedictines, he trained them in the spiritual life, pedagogy, and care of the sick. They quickly decided to deepen their commitment with religious vows and became the Sisters of Mary. In 1964, they opened the first orphanage, the Boystowns and Girlstowns, as Fr. Al dubbed them.

Fr. Al next opened a medical dispensary in the slums. Two others soon followed. He also started Operation Bootstrap, a combined fundraising and work program. In the direct mail campaigns, providing a small gift inspired more donations. The gift was a handkerchief, handstitched with a traditional Korean technique by women from the slums. At its height, the cottage industry employed two thousand people. Accompanying the handkerchief, Fr. Al wrote, "The poor of Korea do not want a handout, they want to work and this is what Operation Bootstrap gives them." By 1967, with a thousand orphans in the care of the Sisters of Mary, he had been relieved of parish work to dedicate all his time to emerging projects. The Sisters had already been visiting the Beggars' Hospice, a poorly run hospital for the most destitute sick that was operated by the city. That year, the city asked Fr. Al and the Sisters to take it over. The death rate dropped dramatically. He was also on the verge of opening a school for slum children, who faced discrimination at the regular public schools.

Near the Beggars' Hospice was the Jaesaengwon Camp, another municipal operation that provided shelter for 1,200 people of all ages. The city had given its management to a man everyone called "Big Daddy." He ran it for his own benefit, mafia-style. The able-bodied were sent out to work and then had their wages stolen by the guards, while children and the disabled were neglected or abused, and the aid supplies coming from different sources were sold on the black market. The sisters had already reported to Fr. Al that they had heard screams coming from it at night. When a young girl from the camp came to the Beggars' Hospice dying of tuberculosis and malnourishment, Fr. Al decided to act. He first sent a report to the public health agency of Busan, but it did nothing. He then wrote to the authorities in Seoul. This led to Big Daddy's arrest, but he was quickly released, having already blackmailed many government officials. Big Daddy and Fr. Al with the Sisters of Mary were now locked in a standoff. Big Daddy first tried to get Fr. Al deported. Then Fr. Al negotiated the release of two hundred boys from the camp into his care. But when Big Daddy couldn't extort everything he wanted from Fr. Al, he attempted to kidnap the priest. A daily runner, Fr. Al couldn't be caught. He countered by bringing formal charges against Big Daddy, but the key witness suddenly disappeared. Finally, to force the government to step in, the Sisters of Mary collected 123,000 signatures in three weeks calling for an investigation. With the situation reaching the attention of ever higher levels of government, the president of Korea ordered a secret investigation that led to arrests and the closure of the camp. Fr. Al built a second orphanage to care for the hundreds of children.

In the 1970s, Fr. Al's work continued to expand. He built two hospitals and replicated his Boystowns and Girlstowns in Seoul. He was also given a facility for disabled men in Seoul to run, which prompted him to form the Brothers of Christ, a community of brothers. In 1982, Cardinal Jaime Sin, archbishop of Manila, convinced him to expand to the Philippines. His work had gained international recognition as well, even a nomination for the Nobel Peace Prize in 1984. Just five years later, he was diagnosed with Amyotrophic Lateral Sclerosis (ALS), also known as Lou Gehrig's disease. Despite his diagnosis, he accepted the invitation to expand to Mexico. The degenerative disease marked the last of years of life with humility and patience. As he was wasting away, he wrote to his sister that he would be happy if his epitaph read "Here lies Fr. Al. He tried his best for Jesus."

He died at the Girlstown in Manila in 1992 and was declared venerable in 2015.

☙

☙

Please report any miracles or favors to:

World Villages for Children
180 Admiral Cochrane Drive, Suite 240
Annapolis, MD 2140
(800) 662-6316
WorldVillages.org
info@worldvillages.org

Chapter 6

Saints of the Future: Servants of God

An incomplete list of all the servants of God from American sainthood causes:

Martyrs of La Florida

> Luis de Cáncer (ca. 1500–1549), Antonio Cuipa (d. 1704) and eighty-four companion martyrs of the "La Florida" Missions (d. 1549–1706), Professed Priests and Religious of the Dominicans, Jesuits, and the Franciscan Friars Minor; Laypeople from the Dioceses of Pensacola-Tallahassee, Orlando, Venice, and St. Augustine (Florida, U.S.)

Martyrs of Virginia

> • Luis de Quirós (d. 1571), Professed Priest of the Jesuits (Cadíz, Spain)
>
> • Gabriel de Solís (d. 1571), Novice of the Jesuits (Spain)
>
> • Juan Bautista Méndez (d. 1571), Novice of the Jesuits (Spain)
>
> • Juan Bautista de Segura (1529–1571), Professed Priest of the Jesuits (Toledo, Spain)
>
> • Gabriel Gómez (d. 1571), Professed Religious of the Jesuits (Granada, Spain)
>
> • Sancho Zeballos (d. 1571), Professed Religious of the Jesuits (Seville, Spain)

- Pedro Mingot Linares (d. 1571), Professed Religious of the Jesuits (Valencia, Spain)
- Cristóbal Redondo (d. 1571), Novice of the Jesuits (Spain)

Martyrs of Georgia

- Pedro de Corpa (ca. 1555–1597), Professed Priest of the Franciscan Friars Minor (Burgos, Spain)
- Blas de Rodríguez (ca. 1500–1597), Professed Priest of the Franciscan Friars Minor (Cáceres, Spain)
- Miguel de Añon (ca. 1550 to 1560–1597), Professed Priest of the Franciscan Friars Minor (Zaragoza, Spain)
- Antonio de Badajoz (ca. 1550–1597), Professed Religious of the Franciscan Friars Minor (Badajoz, Spain)
- Francisco de Beráscola (ca. 1560 to 1570–1597), Professed Religious of the Franciscan Friars Minor (Vizcaya, Spain)

Felice de Andreis (1778–1820), Priest of the Congregation of the Mission (Vincentians) (Cuneo, Italy–Missouri, U.S.)

Magí Catalá Guasch (1761–1830), Professed Priest of the Franciscan Friars Minor (Tarragona, Spain–California, U.S.)

Simon-Guillaume-Gabriel Bruté de Rémur (1779–1839), Bishop of Indianapolis (Ille-et-Vilaine, France–Indiana, U.S.)

Demetrius Augustine Gallitzin (1770–1840), Priest of the Diocese of Altoona-Johnstown (The Hague, Netherlands–Pennsylvania, U.S.)

Giuseppe Rosati (1789–1843), Priest of the Congregation of the Missions (Vincentians); Bishop of Fort Louis (Frosinone, Italy–Missouri, U.S.–Rome, Italy)

Juliette Noel Toussaint (ca. 1786–1851), Married Layperson of the Archdiocese of New York (Haiti–New York, U.S.)

Pierre-Jean-Mathias Loras (1792–1858), Bishop of Dubuque (Lyon, France–Iowa, U.S.)

Martyrs of Shreveport (Louisiana, U.S.):

* Isidore Quémerais (1847–1873), Priest of the Diocese of Shreveport (Ille-et-Vilaine, France)
* Jean Pierre (1831–1873), Priest of the Diocese of Shreveport (Côtes-d'Armor, France)
* Jean-Marie Bilier (1839–1873), Priest of the Diocese of Shreveport (Côtes-d'Armor, France)
* Louis-Marie Gergaud (1832–1873), Priest of the Diocese of Shreveport (Loire-Atlantique, France)
* François Le Vézouët (1833–1873), Priest of the Diocese of Shreveport (Côtes-d'Armor, France)

Patrick Ryan (1845–1878), Priest of the Diocese of Knoxville (Tipperary, Ireland–Tennessee, U.S.)

Mary Elizabeth Lange (ca. 1794–1882), Founder of the Oblate Sisters of Providence (Santiago de Cuba, Cuba–Maryland, U.S.)

Isaac Thomas Hecker (1819–1888), Priest and Founder of the Missionary Society of St. Paul the Apostle (Paulist Fathers) (New York, U.S.)

Joan Adelaide O'Sullivan (María Adelaida of St. Teresa) (1817–1893), Professed Religious of the Discalced Carmelite Nuns (New York, U.S.–León, Spain)

Louis de Goesbriand (1816–1899), Bishop of Burlington (Finistère–Vermont, U.S.)

Anna Bentivoglio (Maria Maddalena of the Sacred Heart of Jesus) (1824–1905), Professed Religious of the Poor Clare Nuns (Rome, Italy–Indiana, U.S.)

Joseph Heinrichs (Leo) (1867–1908), Professed Priest of the Franciscan Friars Minor; Martyr (Heinsberg, Germany–Colorado, U.S.)

Adele-Louise-Marie de Mandat Grancey (1837–1915), Vowed Member of the Daughters of Charity of St. Vincent de Paul (Côte-d'Or, France–Kansas, U.S.–Izmir, Turkey)

Julia Greeley (ca. 1833–1918), Layperson of the Diocese of Denver (Missouri, U.S.–Colorado, U.S.)

Thomas Frederick Price (1860–1919), Priest of the Diocese of Raleigh; Cofounder of the Maryknoll Missionary Society (North Carolina, U.S.–Hong Kong, China)

Francis Joseph Parater (1897–1920), Seminarian of the Diocese of Richmond (Virginia, U.S.–Rome, Italy)

John Eckert (Stephen of Dublin) (1869–1923), Professed Priest of the Franciscan Capuchins (Ontario, Canada–Wisconsin, U.S.)

Jan Cieplak (1857–1926), Apostolic Administrator of Mohilev; Archbishop of Vilnius (Śląskie, Poland–New Jersey, U.S.)

Theresia Ijsseldijk (Theresia of the Holy Trinity) (1897–1926), Professed Religious of the Carmelite Sisters of the Divine Heart of Jesus (Gelderland, Netherlands–Missouri, U.S.)

Rose Hawthorne (Mary Alphonsa) (1851–1926), Founder of the Dominican Sisters of St. Rose of Lima (Dominican Sisters of Hawthorne) (Massachusetts, U.S.–New York, U.S.)

Maria Grazia Bellotti LaPercha (1882–1927), Married Layperson of the Archdiocese of Newark (Potenza, Italy–New Jersey, U.S.)

Federico Salvador Ramón (1867–1931), Priest of the Diocese of Almería; Founder of the Servants of the Immaculate Child Mary (Almería, Spain–California, U.S.)

Ira Barnes Dutton (Joseph) (1843–1931), Layperson of the Diocese of Honolulu; Member of the Secular Franciscans (Vermont, U.S.–Hawaii, U.S.)

James Anthony Walsh (1891–1936), Priest and Cofounder of the Maryknoll Missionary Society; Titular Bishop of Seine-Assuan (Massachusetts, U.S.–New York, U.S.)

Ángel Baraibar Moreno (1891–1936), Priest of the Archdiocese of Toledo; Martyr (San Juan, Puerto Rico–Toledo, Spain)

Anna Marie Lindenberg (Theresa of Jesus) (1887–1939), Professed Religious of the Carmelite Nuns of the Ancient Observance (Münster, Germany–Pennsylvania, U.S.)

Lewis Thomas Wattson (Paul James) (1863–1940), Founder and Professed Priest of the Franciscan Friars of the Atonement (Maryland, U.S.–New York, U.S.)

Bernard John Quinn (1888–1940), Priest of the Diocese of Brooklyn (New Jersey, U.S.–New York, U.S.)

Blandina Segale (1850–1941), Professed Religious of the Sisters of Charity of Cincinnati (Genoa, Italy–Ohio, U.S.)

Joseph Verbis Lafleur (1912–1944), Priest of the Military Ordinariate of the United States (Louisiana, U.S.–Zamboanga de Norte, Philippines)

Edward Joseph Flanagan (1886–1948), Priest of the Archdiocese of Omaha (Roscommon, Ireland–Nebraska, U.S.–Berlin, Germany)

Rhoda Wise (1888–1948), Married Layperson of the Diocese of Youngstown (Ohio, U.S.)

Nicholas Black Elk (1863–1950), Married Layperson of the Diocese of Grand Rapids (Wyoming, U.S.–South Dakota, U.S.)

James Maginn (1911–1950), Priest of the Missionary Society of St. Columban; Martyr (Montana, U.S.–Gangwon, South Korea)

They Might Be Saints

Patrick Brennan (1901–1950), Priest of the Missionary Society of St. Columban; Vicar Apostolic of Kwangju; Martyr (Illinois, U.S.–Daejeon, South Korea)

Emil Joseph Kapaun (1916–1951), Priest of the Diocese of Wichita (Kansas, U.S.–North Korea)

Francis Xavier Ford (1892–1952), Priest of the Maryknoll Missionary Society; Bishop of Kaiying (New York, U.S.–Guangdong, China)

Julia Teresa Tallon (Mary Teresa) (1867–1954), Founder of the Parish Visitors of Mary Immaculate (New York, U.S.)

Mary Virginia Merrick (1866–1955), Layperson of the Archdiocese of Washington D.C.; Founder of the Christ Child Society (Washington D.C., U.S.)

Cora Louise Yorgason Evans (1904–1957), Married Layperson of the Diocese of Monterrey (Utah, U.S.–California, U.S.)

Teresa Kearney (Mary Kevin) (1875–1957), Founder of the Little Sisters of St. Francis and the Franciscan Missionary Sisters for Africa (Wicklow, Ireland–Jinja, Uganda–Massachusetts, U.S.)

Luigi Sturzo (1871–1959), Priest of the Diocese of Caltagirone (Caltagirone, Italy–London, England–New York, U.S.–Rome, Italy)

Charlene Marie Richard (1947–1959), Child of the Diocese of Lafayette (Louisiana, U.S.)

Vincent Robert Capodanno (1929–1967), Priest of the Maryknoll Missionary Society; Priest of the Military Ordinariate of the United States (New York, U.S.–Quàng Nam, Vietnam)

Jean Martin Eyraud (1880–1968), Priest of the Archdiocese of New Orleans (Haute Alpes, France–Louisiana, U.S.)

Giancarlo Rastelli (1933–1970), Married Layperson of the Diocese of Parma (Pescara, Italy–Minnesota, U.S.)

William Evans (1919–1971), Professed Priest of the Congregation of Holy Cross (Massachusetts, U.S.–Dhaka, Bangladesh)

Ernő Tindira (1892–1972), Priest of the Diocese of Mukacheve of the Latins; Martyr (Pennsylvania, U.S.–Mukacheve, Ukraine)

Daniel Foley (Theodore of Mary Immaculate) (1913–1974), Professed Priest of the Passionists (Massachusetts, U.S.–Rome, Italy)

Michael Jerome Cypher (Casimir) (1941–1975), Professed Priest of Franciscan Conventuals; Martyr (Wisconsin, U.S.–Olancho, Honduras)

Paul Michael Murphy (1939–1976), Layperson of the Diocese of Phoenix; Consecrated Member of the Miles Jesu (Illinois, U.S.–Arizona, U.S.)

Auguste [Nonco] Pelafigue (1888–1977), Layperson of the Diocese of Lafayette; Member of the Apostleship of Prayer League (Haute-Pyrénées, France–Louisiana, U.S.)

George Willmann (1920–1977), Professed Priest of the Jesuits (New York, U.S.–Manila, Philippines)

Dorothy Day (1897–1980), Layperson of the Archdiocese of New York; Founder of the Catholic Worker Movement (New York, U.S.)

Juan Luis Ellacuria Echevarría (Aloysius) (1905–1981), Professed Priest of the Claretians (Vizcaya, Spain–California, U.S.)

William Slattery (1895–1982), Priest of the Congregation of the Mission (Vincentians) (Maryland, U.S.–Pennsylvania, U.S.)

Vincent Joseph McCauley (1906–1982), Professed Priest of the Congregation of Holy Cross; Archbishop of Fort Portal (Iowa U.S.–Minnesota, U.S.–Kampala, Uganda)

José Luis Múzquiz de Miguel [Joseph Múzquiz] (1912–1983), Priest of the Personal Prelature of the Holy Cross and Opus Dei (Badajoz, Spain–Massachusetts, U.S.)

Terence James Cooke (1921–1983), Archbishop of New York;
  Cardinal (New York, U.S.)

Walter Ciszek (1904–1984), Professed Priest of the Jesuits (Pennsylvania, U.S.–New York, U.S.)

John Maronic (1922–1985), Professed Priest of the Missionary
  Oblates of Mary Immaculate; Founder of the Victorious Missionaries (Minnesota, U.S.–Illinois, U.S.)

Gabriel Wilhelmus Manek (1913–1989), Professed Priest of the
  Society of the Divine Word; Archbishop of Endeh; Founder of
  the Daughters of Our Lady Queen of the Holy Rosary (Nusa
  Tenggara Timur, Indonesia–Colorado, U.S.)

Thea Bowman (1937–1990), Professed Religious of the Franciscan Sisters of Perpetual Adoration (Mississippi, U.S.)

María Belen Guzmán Florit (Dominga) (1897–1993), Founder
  of the Dominican Sisters of Fátima (San Juan, Puerto Rico–
  Ponce, Puerto Rico)

John Joseph McKniff (1907–1994), Professed Priest of the Augustinians (Pennsylvania, U.S.–Florida, U.S.–Piura, Peru)

Rossella Petrellese (1972–1994), Layperson of the Diocese of
  Acerra (Naples, Italy–Minnesota, U.S.)

Gabriel Gonsum Ganaka (1937–1999), Archbishop of Jos (Pla-
  teau, Nigeria–New York, U.S.)

Ida Peterfy (1922–2000), Founder of the Society Devoted to the
  Sacred Heart (Košice, Slovakia–California, U.S.)

Gertrude Agnes Barber (1911–2000), Layperson of the Diocese
  of Erie (Pennsylvania, U.S.)

John Anthony Hardon (1914–2000), Professed Priest of the
  Jesuits (Pennsylvania, U.S.–Michigan, U.S.)

Leonard LaRue (Marinus) (1914–2001), Professed Religious of
  the Benedictines (Ottilien Congregatian) (Pennsylvania–
  New Jersey, U.S.)

Gwen Cecilia Billings Conicker (1939–2002), Married Layperson of the Diocese of Steubenville; Cofounder of the Apostolate for Family Consecration (Illinois, U.S.–Ohio, U.S.)

Joseph Henry Cappel (1908–2004), Priest of the Maryknoll Missionary Society (Kentucky, U.S.–Talca, Chile)

Maria Esperanza Medrano Parra de Bianchini (1928–2004), Married Layperson of the Dioceses of Los Teques and Metuchen (Monagas, Venezuela–New Jersey, U.S.)

Fernando Rielo Pardal (1923–2004), Layperson of the Archdiocese of Madrid; Founder of the Idente Missionaries of Christ the Redeemer (Madrid, Spain–New York, U.S.)

Joseph Walijewski (1914–2006), Priest of the Diocese of La Crosse (Michigan, U.S.–Lima, Peru)

William Edward Atkinson (1946–2006), Professed Priest of the Augustinians (Pennsylvania, U.S.)

Irving Charles Houle (Francis) (1925–2009), Married Layperson of the Diocese of Marquette (Michigan, U.S.)

About the Author

Michael O'Neill is an award-winning author, EWTN Radio and television host, and creator of the popular miracle-tracking website MiracleHunter.com, cited worldwide in news articles and books, including renowned Mariologist Fr. René Laurentin's comprehensive work *The Dictionary of the Apparitions of the Virgin Mary*.

O'Neill, a graduate of Stanford University and a member of the Mariological Society of America and the Theological Commission of the International Marian Association, has been interviewed about his research numerous times for features on Catholic television programs and in secular media, such as *NBC Today*, *The Dr. Oz Show*, and the History Channel. He was the consultant for the *National Geographic* December 2015 cover story about the Virgin Mary, "The Most Powerful Woman in the World," and was interviewed as the Marian expert on the corresponding television piece for *National Geographic Explorer*. O'Neill served as the expert commentator during the 2010 live broadcast of the first Marian apparition approval in history at Champion, Wisconsin, and during EWTN's coverage at the hundredth-anniversary Mass of the apparitions of Our Lady of Fátima. He is the host of the weekly Relevant Radio program *The*

Miracle Hunter and a frequent contributor to *The Drew Mariani Show*.

His books include *Exploring the Miraculous* (Our Sunday Visitor, 2015), *365 Days with Mary* (Salt Media, 2016), *20 Answers: Apparitions & Revelations* (Catholic Answers Press, 2017), and *Virgin, Mother, Queen* (Ave Maria Press, 2019). O'Neill was the co-host of the television special *Miracle Hunters* (UpTV, 2015) and was a panelist for the twelve-part television series *Mary, Mother of All* (Shalom World TV, 2017). He is the creator and host of the EWTN docuseries *They Might Be Saints*, on the lives of future American saints and the search for canonization miracles. His EWTN travel series *Explore with the Miracle Hunter* examines the places of Catholicism's most famous miracles.